I Found GOD In Kyancutta

The story of one woman's relationship with God

PETRA KELLY

Published by Petra Kelly

Copyright © 2024. All rights reserved. No portion of this publication may be used, reproduced or transmitted by any means, digital, electronic, mechanical, photocopy or recording without written permission of the publisher, except in the case of brief quotations within critical articles or reviews.

ISBN: 978-1-7636965-0-1

First edition, 2024

For book orders and enquiries, contact: kellypetra25@gmail.com

A catalogue record for this book is available from the National Library of Australia

Dedication

To my beloved family

Silver and gold have I none; but what I have I give to you... Acts 3:6

Where My Story Starts

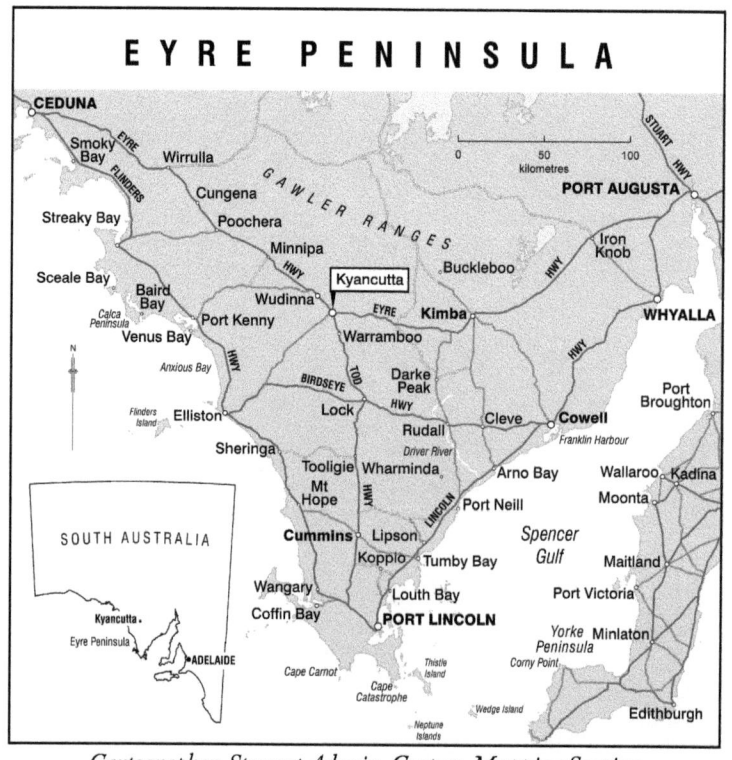

Cartographer: Stewart Adrain, Custom Mapping Services

Contents

Guiding Scripture 1	1
Guiding Scripture 2	2
The Commission	3
1. Setting the Scene	4
2. A Few Other Explanations	12
Before I Entered Time and Space	21
3. Growing Up	22
Stepping Stones 1	31
4. Hungry for More	32
5. Finding God in Kyancutta	36
A Few Words About Jesus	40
6. More About Jesus	41
He Knows Us	55
7. Early Lessons	56
... and by the way Petra...	73
8. On Leaving	74

Do Not Store up Treasures on Earth	89
9. In the Thick of it	90
Stepping Stones 2	100
In the Beginning	101
10. Why Include a Chapter About Creation?	102
11. Thirsty	116
Losing My Way	127
12. Things That Helped Me Heal	128
Coming Home	146
13. The Search for Love and Identity	147
Shout for Joy	162
14. Our Purpose	163
15. Finale	169
Bibliography	171

Guiding Scripture 1

How then, can they call on the one they have not believed in?

And how can they believe in the one of whom they have not heard?

And how can they hear without someone preaching to them?

And how can they preach unless they are sent?

As it is written, "How beautiful are the feet of those who bring good news!"

Romans 10:14-15

Guiding Scripture 2

We will tell the next generation the praiseworthy deeds of the Lord,

His power, and the wonders he has done.

He decreed statutes for Jacob and established the law in Israel,

Which he commanded our forefathers to teach their children,

So the next generation would know them,

Even the children yet to be born,

and they in turn would tell their children.

Then they would put their trust in God

And would not forget his deeds but would keep his commands.

Psalm 78:4-7

The Commission

September 2022

I was listening to this song: *Jesus my Lord, my God my all,*

How can I love thee as I ought?

And how revere this wondrous gift

So far surpassing hope or joy? I asked: What can I do to love you?

He answered:

> *Write about how you have been able to turn to me again and again even in times of wilful disobedience -and you have been met with love and mercy. That is who I am - all love, all mercy. And yes, all mystery, (but) you cannot write about that. Not yet. I ease people's suffering. I cannot remove it. Just as the western world provides weapons for Ukraine, they are not saving Ukraine from their peril but they are providing a network of support and resources. All one needs is the will to fight on and I will provide all that is necessary to walk with love and dignity through all manner of trials. Let others wrestle with the logic of the invisible God. You just tell your story as it is, unvarnished.*

Chapter One

Setting the Scene

God Talks to Me

I'm an average person. You wouldn't notice me in a crowd. I wasn't ever the smartest person in the room and certainly not the most beautiful. Nor was I exceptionally gifted in sport. At best I held my own in the classroom and on the tennis court. I wasn't highly athletic but I could run enough to make it into the relay teams for my age group but never as the final runner. I made the debating team but never as third speaker. I have always hovered close to the middle. Even in personality tests, I hover near the middle of the introversion/extroversion continuums.

Nor am I especially holy. Although I read that money doesn't make you happy, I don't quite believe it. I'm sure it would make me happy. I give to the poor but I do not give my all. Although I profess to be a follower of Jesus Christ, I enjoy the comforts of middle-class life in the western world. I am not an ascetic. I have not read widely. I have not searched multiple traditions to find truth or enlightenment. I have not gone off to the east to find that special teacher. I have not renounced much at all, so in my mind I'm not exactly a likely candidate for special attention from the Divine. And yet God talks to me. You need to know this because my story is full of words that I believe God has spoken directly to me, not just out of the Bible but directly to me, even when I didn't deserve his help.

I'm a follower, not a leader. All my life I have found decisions hard to make. I wait for instructions. I am not especially brave. I am not a trail blazer. I wait and wait. I pray and pray. I am so reluctant to make the first move. I want the other party to make the first move. I stayed for a long time unhappy in my marriage because I was waiting to be saved. God would help us even though countless counselling sessions hadn't been able to. I was not about to give up because I'd made those forever marriage vows. But I fell out of love and it doesn't really matter why. We seemed unable to grow together anymore. I was, I am human and I failed at the long haul of love. Maybe it would have been better for everyone if I had left earlier but fearful and unskilled in personal decision making, I stayed. Waiting and expecting God to save me - save us. It was a weak exit. And although my leaving seemed in total contradiction to God's laws, God did not abandon me then either. God kept talking to me.

As I said, I'm not a super religious or spiritual person. I struggle with all the usual distractions in life. I like things and as far as my means allow me, I am a dedicated consumer. I think I've lived a relatively small life. I can't point to great achievements, bold plans, legacy. My footprint has been small. Growing up in a small country town, I remember when I first realised that another world even existed beyond the low line of hills that flanked our western horizon. I was standing outside staring westward and was excited knowing some older sisters would soon be returning from boarding school for school holidays. Maybe I was six or seven at the time. On that day, my brain finally computed that they lived in a bigger world than mine. They were out there in that other world living their lives, even as I stood small on the footpath of an obscure town.

Nor despite the smallness of my life, have I tried to change its trajectory. I have not aspired to greatness. I've followed a modest path - with average achievements - and average failures - putting one foot in front of the other even in the dark times. If anything, my greatest achievement has been that I've been able to keep putting that one foot in front of the other. So, there's no reason to think I especially deserved a hot line to heaven. And yet God talks to me.

How does God talk to me? According to my Christian beliefs, I have three persons in God to consider, the Father, the Son and the Holy Spirit. When I do hear, or when I do have interventions from the other side, what does God say to me and which God do I hear from? I accept they are limited names and some say, heavily biased by patriarchal history. Who knows how gender applies to the Divine. *"God created man in his own image, in his own image he created him; male and female he created them"* Genesis 1:27. So God must therefore share both male and female characteristics. Eager to know more about God, one of the disciples, Philip, asks Jesus to show him the Father. Jesus answers him, with I think, just a touch of exasperation:

"Don't you know me Philip, even after I have been among you such a long time? Anyone who has seen me has seen the Father" John 14:9.

Jesus, as he is described in the gospels, and as verified by other documentary evidence of the day, was undoubtedly a man. There can be no confusion about that. However once in the streets of Sydney someone approached me on the footpath and I couldn't tell at all which gender they were. I thought at the time - there goes the face of God.

What is it like hearing from the other side? Communication is a better word to use than hearing from or speaking or listening to. In English language studies, teachers refer to the four macro skills: reading, writing, listening and speaking. We can certainly 'get a message', receive direction from God from what we read. Pre-eminently the Bible is the revealed word of God to the world and so regular reading of scripture is a sure and safe way to hear from God. That's one way I hear from God.

I don't always know who of the three are communicating with me. I don't hear a voice saying, 'hi this is God the Father speaking'. Or 'good morning, Petra, it's the Holy Spirit today - Jesus and his dad are busy so you've got me.' It's nothing like that. Sometimes I have no reason to think about which person of the Trinity is communicating with me. But usually, I know from the context who it is. For example, I'm swimming at the beach, delighting in the cold-water waves that are hitting me, taking my breath away and regularly pushing me under. I say spontaneously to Jesus, I guess body surfing was something you never got to do when you were on earth? Quick as a flash an answer came back:

Ah yes, but I walked on water.

Clearly, I could tell Jesus was communicating with me that time.

The Bible is a sure and safe way to hear from God. However, there are no limits to the ways God can communicate with us. One day I was taking a walk outside in my lunch hour, deeply troubled, anxious and afraid about what seemed to me at that post-divorce time, an insecure future. I saw these words being written in the sky by a random plane flying over the suburb where I worked: NO OTHER NAME. I knew there were many places in scripture that refer to God in this way and I had no doubt they were direct words for me, pointing me back to having faith in Jesus.

"Salvation is found in no one else, for there is no other name under heaven given to men by which we must be saved" Acts 4:12.

However, in the main, God and others who have communicated with me from the other side, seem able to bypass the four macro skills easily enough. They have their own special communication skill, some kind of thought transfer perhaps. This is how it works for me. Sometimes I receive messages when I am consciously seeking direction. Other times they arrive unexpectedly when I'm not asking or seeking anything at all; they just arrive as a surprise insight or a thought that cuts through whatever moment I am living in and I am instantly changed by it.

For example, I'm in the supermarket. I'm thinking about the lunch I am going to buy. For context, for several weeks I'd been wrestling with the question about what Covid vaccine to take. I had just become eligible for getting one of two vaccines that were available at that time and so the question had a new urgency to it. One was considered preferable but that one wasn't available for my age group. I really didn't want to take the other one which already had some risks associated with it. The media had been full of the debate. As I bent forward to check the food in the display cabinet, not thinking of vaccines at all, this message arrived:

Do you think I am in charge?

I instantly knew the context this question was referring to. And it wasn't about my choice of lunch. I do believe God is in charge of my life and the timing of my death and so what was I worried about? It wasn't a totally unambiguous direction - I mean it wasn't as clear as, "take vaccine A or B and you'll be fine" But I knew from that message, that simple question, *'Do you think I am in charge?',* that if it was my time to die then I might be one of those rare people who died because of a vaccine related complication but I did not need to fear that. I could relax and trust that God was in charge of the time of my death. I haven't had a moment of doubt since then - about the vaccine that is.

Or another time: pre-divorce, I was outside my home on the farm, enjoying a quiet time and reflecting on the first few verses from Psalm 19.

"The heavens declare the glory of God;

The skies proclaim the work of his hands.

Day after day they pour forth speech;

Night after night they display knowledge.

There is no speech or language where their voice is not heard."

Whilst looking out over the beauty of the nearby landscape, I was marvelling at the incredible intimacy Father God offers us in relationship. I wasn't asking for anything in particular. It was late in the day. I could hear beautiful music playing from inside the house. My arms opened wide to the heavens and this is what I heard:

> *My intimacy is spread out all around you. I have exposed myself, made myself vulnerable in the landscape; given myself, opened myself to you. I am here, surrounding you, close, very close, open, outstretched.*

Everything shone with a new beauty. The fullness of God is in everything – available, still, waiting, loving, longing for relationship with us far more than we for him. The rim of the nearby stubble paddock spread out around me, glowing gold in the dusk of late summer, gleaming still despite the looming darkness. Spread like an invitation, still, still, so still and warm and loving me. There is no end to the presence of God. No beginning, no end. He is.

As I write about my developing life with God, I will describe many such instances of direct Divine communication. In all cases, after these interventions arrive, my mood, my understanding of whatever issue I am dealing with can pivot dramatically. Sometimes I hear distinct exact words, as in *"Do you think I am in charge?"* Well that's not exactly true,

I don't 'hear', as in through my ears, but words and sometimes whole sentences arrive in my mind. Divine communication is much more economical. Words are just there, having bypassed the intricate workings of my human physical inner ear.

Sometimes I see a scene unfolding in my mind that I can watch take place. Again, this is not a seeing experience that uses the incredible engineering design that connects our physical eyes to our brains and produces our sight. As with hearing, this kind of seeing bypasses the physical mechanisms and arrives by some other modality into an understanding in my mind. Sometimes I am both in the scene and I am the watcher. As the scene unfolds, I experience it emotionally and am changed because of it - enlightened, inspired or just left full of awe and wonder and love. At other times, understanding arrives in a more nuanced way. I just know about something. I know what action I need to take. I know how to resolve whatever my current situation or dilemma is. The direction or answer is just there for me to take, to absorb and maybe to apply. Or if there is no clear direction, I am content to accept non-direction. I am at peace with not knowing and I go ahead and do whatever I think is best.

This acceptance of 'not knowing' was a lesson God tried to teach me early in my new walk with him when I used to ask for answers about everything. God interjected essentially to remind me that I could learn to be guided more intuitively by his Spirit rather than ask incessantly for direction about every single step. At the time I had been asking something ridiculously simple: should I go out or stay at home tonight? He answered me:

> *Listen, listen, listen to me my child! Grow more sensitive to the promptings of my Spirit, that is my voice, the voice which is speaking constantly to you. These words are but an echo of what I have already written upon your heart. How often it is that you do not hear. Perfect communion is unspoken; it is found in silence. Ask me to teach you about this silent communion. There is purity and a directness in silence. You will come to know the joy of it.*

At other times I might have been searching for insight. I may even have been journalling in an effort to sort my own thoughts out. If a message comes then, when I have a pen in my hand, I start writing down what I am receiving. Whole paragraphs emerge on the page. I can't get them down fast enough.

Always after one of these interventions from the other side, many of which I will describe in detail as my story unfolds, I am taken out of whatever small circle of thinking I have been caught in. Always I am left feeling softened. In some way the space in my heart is bigger. I can rise up, move on ... lighter, calmer and always empowered to give a more loving response and/or get to sleep!

This has been a very good thing across the course of my life because my journals often show my raw unprocessed first responses. These first responses are not always kind or loving. However by the time I get to live out my responses in the real world, by then my communication is usually kinder and less damaging than my first journalled words would have been. I feel immensely grateful for this guidance, this easy access to the resources from the heart of the Divine.

And by the way, it's not just God who communicates with me. Over the years I have had people who have died communicate with me. I don't invite this. I don't want to engage with bad spirits. That is expressly forbidden. However when they do arrive, these saints from the other side, I am open and alert and I listen.

The apostle Paul teaches in 1 Timothy 2:5 that there is *"one mediator between God and men, the man Christ Jesus."* But he also begins that chapter by exhorting the brethren *"I urge, then first of all, that requests, prayers, intercession and thanksgiving, be made for everyone"*. We who believe in Jesus are members of one body, and I have been taught to believe that those of us here now on earth and those who have died in Christ are all members of this same body.

"Therefore, since we are surrounded by such a great cloud of witnesses" Hebrews 12:1.

The veil is thin. Many Christians believe that you should always go straight to God. No intermediaries are required they say. I say in reply, yet you are happy enough to ask each other to pray for you and that's not going straight to God, is it? So, what's the difference with me asking those who have died to pray for me? The veil is so thin. I'm grateful I have been taught to trust and use this avenue of intercessory prayer.

Over the years it's become clear to me that there are boundaries to the kinds of information or encouragement that I receive from God or from those who have died. I rarely receive insights into the lives of others. I receive no special insights into the great mysteries of the world. Communication that comes to me is usually only about me.

Now that I have established this fact – that I hear direct messages from God, I need to explain a few other things so that you will better understand my story.

Chapter Two

A Few Other Explanations

One: This is not a light-hearted story.

Flotsam and Jetsam[1]

A word, a look, a phrase, moments in time continually beach themselves on the shore of my mind

I collect them involuntarily like flotsam and jetsam

Then I pick over them, prodding gingerly, exploring, rolling them around in my mind and heart,

Like new flavours on the tongue

Then I spread them out in words, gossamer fine

For time to add its perspective

Cool down, you said (nicely)

---

1. Flotsam and jetsam are the debris that washes up on beaches.

Meaning – lighten up

I think

You could as well ask the snow to melt on Everest

You know, I look at the Crocodile Dundees[2]

Sometimes quizzically, sometime enviously

I don't know their rhythms; I can't sing their songs

I seem to be

Forever tuned differently

And that is both

My gift

And my burden

I've been encouraged to 'lighten up' many times throughout my life and I wrote the above piece in response to one such time. But I am not a light-hearted person. I do exactly what my poem describes, I pour over everything that comes my way - from every angle.

Perhaps that's why I love comedy so much, it provides the balance that I can't seem to find within myself. I love 30 Rock and The Big Bang, even though I don't subscribe to that as an origin of the world theory. I love Schitt's Creek, Superstore and Brooklyn Nine-Nine. I do watch dramas, plenty of them but I prefer to end an evening laughing along with Ted Lasso or the cast of The Good Life.

I don't get jokes easily. The funniest thing about me is that I often have to have jokes explained to me or I get the joke late and start to laugh after every one else has finished laughing! So this story of my life with God was never going to be light-hearted. It unfolds just as my life has, intensely. If you ask me was I ever happy, I would say yes, probably many

---

2. I use this term, as a metaphor for people who can be light-hearted, casual and even cheerful no matter what life throws at them.

times but then I would have to launch into a definition of what happiness really means. I am grateful for my life. I have lived in a privileged era of peace and plenty in my part of the world. I have not had to worry about survival. I've tasted joy, deep joy. I've loved and been loved. I'm one of the lucky ones. Nevertheless, the story of my life with God is not a rollicking, happy go lucky tale.

Two: I am not going to write about all the details of my life. There is nothing so special about my life that warrants that level of scrutiny. And frankly, it would be boring! My aim in avoiding a detailed chronological approach, is to keep the focus on the main character – God and his interventions and loving interactions with me. That is the gold in my journals.

Three: Stepping-Stones. When I do jump across some of my life's time zones in order to omit irrelevant details, I will indicate this by using the term 'Stepping-Stones' accompanied with brief dot points.

Four: I use four main names when referring to God: God, the Father, Jesus and the Holy Spirit.

Five: The most important book I refer to throughout is the Bible. Scripture quotations are italicised, bracketed with quotation marks and keep full line length. I use the New International Version (NIV) translation unless otherwise stated. God's direct words to me, are italicised, unbracketed and unless very short – they are indented and justified.

Six: Privacy. Inevitably other people's lives are intertwined with mine. I have an extensive circle of friends and family, siblings, children, and grandchildren. I am truly grateful for all who have passed through my world. Thank you for your contributions. As I share my journey about my life with God, my intention is to honour the privacy of others. I hope to do that respectfully. So, in the main, I will be sharing only God's dealings and messages as they pertain directly to me.

Seven: I am a non-aligned Christian. I was brought up by parents who observed the traditions of the Catholic Church and I am grateful for the foundations they provided me and for that reason, I do describe in some detail many of the early steps of my Catholic life. Along the way, I have also belonged to other Christian communities that have helped me grow in my knowledge and experience of God.

I know the apostle Paul, writing in his letters to the early Christians, encourages believers to meet together regularly: *"Therefore encourage one another and build each other up,"* 1 Thessalonians 5:11. But at the moment, I'm not sure where I belong. I'm a work in progress, on my way home to God. All I can testify about is how God, despite my human frailties, has found me, and touched my life over and over again, with incredibly consistent, undeserved love, forgiveness and encouragement.

If you haven't already found this God for yourself then maybe as you read my story, your curiosity will be awakened and you will find God too. Or if your first love for God has waned maybe you will be encouraged to dive back in again and recommit your life to loving and serving this most amazing God.

"Ask, and it shall be given to you; seek, and you will find; knock, and the door will be opened to you" Matthew Ch 7:7.

My Journals

Since my mid-twenties I've kept journals. It's only because of them that I have accurate records to draw from for this telling of my story. Mostly I would write in lined exercise books but if caught with the urge to write outside my home, I would scrawl things down on any scrap of paper that I could find. I've ended up with boxes full of my words.

But I'm getting older. Do I really want my children to be burdened with all those words after I die? To what end? For what purpose? The more I asked the question of myself, the more I thought I should get rid of them. But I don't like getting rid of anything I've written; two rejected manuscripts in my top-drawer attest to that. And so along with my journals, they also remain amongst my papers.

So what's in these journals? Evidence of decades of free therapy. Words help me make sense of my life. Words make me happy. They pour easily out of me onto the page. They clarify, they illuminate. They shake the dust from my soul. They set me back on my feet. They give me life and hope. But those words have not always been edifying. I have seven children and more than double that number of grandchildren as I write this. Why would I want to expose them to all of that!

My journals also record the development of my relationship with God. Since I became a Christian in my mid-twenties, they reflect how I've complained to God, badgered God for certain outcomes, railed angrily against God when things didn't turn out the way I wanted. They reflect how I've asked for help and guidance, expressed thanks and gratitude, and praised and worshipped God. They show me at my best and at my worst.

When I first read the story of the Israelites as they wandered in the desert for all those years, before God finally let them go into the land he had promised them, I was so critical of them. How could they complain against and disobey God? After all, they had firsthand knowledge of the miracles that Moses and Aaron performed in order to get Pharoah to release them from captivity. They had experienced the opening of the Red Sea, followed by the destruction of Pharoah's army as the waters fell back over them. They had experienced the presence of God falling on them as a cloud by day to shelter them from the burning heat of the desert sun and a pillar of fire to warm them by night. On top of all these amazing signs and wonders, throughout their long time in the desert, God supplied them with an amazing food source – manna. They had seen all of this with their own eyes, and yet still they complained. We should have stayed in Egypt they said:

"If only we had meat to eat! We remember the fish we ate in Egypt at no cost – also the cucumbers, melons, leeks, onion and garlic...... we never see anything but this manna!" Numbers 11:4-6.

God did get angry with them – so did Moses but although there were severe consequences for their rebellions, God didn't wipe them out. He met their failures with grace and mercy time and time again.

I am an Israelite. My life is just as theirs, a series of stops and starts, seasons of rebellion followed by seasons of repentance. There's so much then and now that I am not proud of, so much time I've wasted arguing with God! But no matter what I brought to God in prayer, I've always come away comforted, loved, encouraged and often, corrected. On many occasions I've received messages back from God, direct answers that have deeply changed my state of mind and heart. God is indeed, *"our refuge and our strength, an ever-present help in times of trouble"* Psalm 46:1. Perhaps those parts of my journals would be worth saving.

I think only the God-story can help us make sense of this troubled and yet glorious world in which we live, where there seems to be as much pain and suffering as sweet success and joy. This is the reason I want to share what I have *"heard and known"*, *Psalm 78:3* about God, and his *"praiseworthy deeds"*, *Psalm 78:4*. I want my children, grandchildren and children in my family yet to be born, to be confident enough to put their trust in this same God that I have come to know, no matter what is happening in the world around them.

And so I began to reread my journals, harvesting what I thought was of any value.

Underpinning Assumptions

Finally, I believe in the Bible, all of it. If there is something that I stumble across that I can't understand, and I can't find answers from sources I trust, then I accept that is because of my limited earthly understanding. It's not about the character of God.

The Bible consists of 66 separate books written over a period of about 1,500 years, by about forty different writers ranging from Kings to fishermen. It is many things including history, poetry, theology and romance.[3] It tells us the true history of our world, and God's dealings with humankind described largely through the lens of his dealings with one nation, the nation of Israel. Despite its diverse authorship, it claims to be the inspired word of the one true God.

"All scripture is breathed out by God and profitable for teaching, for reproof, for correction, and for training in righteousness so that the man of God may be thoroughly equipped for every good work" 2 Timothy 3:16-17.

However scholars don't always agree about everything that is found in the Bible. Some theologians say many stories in the Bible are allegorical, meaning they should not be taken literally. Others, for example Sarfati in his commentary on Genesis 1-11, acknowledge that the Bible does use linguistic devices such as poetry, metaphor and allegory but that we should be able to know where allegory and metaphor are used from the context. He goes on to say we shouldn't need a *"magic decoder ring"*. (Although I'm pretty sure a decoding device would help me with the book of Revelation!) We should, says Sarfati, largely be able to take what we read in the Bible at face value.[4] This is my approach. I am not a Bible

---

3. (Sarfati et al., 2008) p.36

4. ibid p. 39

scholar and yet I approach the Bible confidently believing that since it is God's Word to humankind, he would have intended ordinary people like me to understand it.

There are other debates about the Bible. For example can we be sure who authored which books and when? And how can the accuracy of early texts be established when variations across the centuries can be found? For example what did Jesus actually say as he was dying on the cross? Did he say, *"Father forgive them for they know not what they do?"* (only recorded in Luke) or was he so caught up in pain and agony that he could only cry out and say, *"My God, my God why have you forsaken me?"* (as recorded in Matthew and Mark) These questions might interest scholars but they don't have to erode our faith in the inerrancy of the Bible.

So having made it clear that I accept the Bible as a literal account of our history, I believe we were created by God: *"So God created man in his own image, in the image of God he created him, male and female he created them"* Genesis 1:27. I believe we were created along with the elements, all matter and space and every other living creature, to share in the life of God, in the fullness of the one, yet three-personned God, Father, Son and Holy Spirit. God being love, wanted to share the glory of his creation with more than the trees and the animals and so he created Adam and Eve *'in his own image'*. They were invited to walk and talk daily in the garden in friendship with this God. What an amazing invitation.

But the disobedience of our forefathers, Adam and Eve, when they ate the fruit from the tree of knowledge of good and evil against God's specific instructions had consequences, shocking consequences that have reverberated down through the ages.

All that had been on offer to humankind, was lost. That's the penalty of disobedience, of sin. And that's what all of us who are descended from Adam and Eve have inherited. That's why there is so much suffering and pain in our world. It wasn't that way in the beginning.

Not many people talk publicly about sin in our western culture. It's not acceptable anymore. It may give offense. We live in a post Christian world. We have moved away from a society based on God's laws as given to us through the prophet Moses and perfected in the teachings of Jesus. We live now in a rights-based culture; 'human rights' have taken over as the source of truth and goodness. And in our western democratic world, how these rights are defined can change from generation to generation. There is no longer such a thing as immutable truth or agreement about what constitutes moral behaviour. So we never talk about sin and yet for those with eyes to see, we are surrounded by it.

This is a problem for Christians. How can we hold to our own Bible-based views without causing offense to those around us? Unless giving offense is inevitable as John 15:19 seems to suggest.

"If you belonged to the world, it would love you as its own. As it is, you do not belong to the world, but I have chosen you out of the world. That is why the world hates you."

Without even opening our mouths, we can be accused of judging others. The New Testament is full of warnings about the dangers of judging others. *"Do not judge or you too will be judged" Matthew 7:1*. And Jesus goes on to spell it out even more clearly: *"You hypocrite, first take the plank out of your own eye, then you will see clearly to remove the speck from your brother's eye" Matthew 7:5.*

It's clear from scripture that there is only one Judge, God himself.

"Then all the trees of the forest will sing for joy,

They will sing before the Lord, for he comes,

He comes to judge the earth.

He will judge the world in righteousness

And the peoples in his truth" Psalm 96:12-13.

Jesus made it clear during the years of his public ministry that he loved and welcomed everyone, but he was also not afraid to tell people to turn away from sin.[5] I humbly acknowledge that I still have much to learn about how to hold firm to my own beliefs without conveying judgement to those whose beliefs and lifestyles may differ from mine.

Despite our propensity towards sinful behaviours, so great is the love of God our Father that he has not left us without hope and without a way back to him. His loving invitation to walk in friendship has never been rescinded. He always had the solution in place,

---

5. John 5:14 and John 8:11

another way to draw us back to himself. To defeat the consequences of sin and death, a price had to be paid. God's perfect sense of justice had to be satisfied. A payment, a sacrifice, a perfect sacrifice had to be found.

What a shocking moment in time it must have been, when in the perfect presence of each other, the sweet unity of the Trinity, bowed before their solution; the Son would be the perfect sacrifice. He would pay the price. What surrender, what impossible love. And so we have the story of the Messiah, the Saviour, woven throughout the Old Testament. Through the mouths of the prophets, God began to reveal the path, the way back, the door through which we could walk back to him, unimpeded by the obstacles of sin and death. The entire purpose of the life of Jesus, fully man and fully God, was to be this sacrifice, to pay this price. Through his death on the cross, Jesus defeated death. Through his perfect sacrifice, we are saved, redeemed, bought back.

"But he was pierced for our transgressions,

He was crushed for our iniquities

The punishment that brought us peace was upon him,

And by his wounds we are healed" Isaiah 53:5.

We are not promised an easy ride but if we surrender our lives to him, we can walk with confidence through all manner of challenges. We do not need to be anxious about a thing. *"I have told you these things, so that in me you may have peace. In this world you will have trouble. But take heart! I have overcome the world."* Jesus' words in John 16:33. This is the version of the history of the world that I subscribe to and which is reflected in the telling of my God story.

So now you know I hear from God, you know my story is not going to follow the pattern of a traditional memoir, and you know that I believe everything in the Bible, now, I can begin to tell my story.

Before I Entered Time and Space

Learned books credit the unborn child in their mother's womb with a level of knowing, but I have even earlier recollections of that time, that pulling away, that tearing of the fragile lace of the space that was to become me, that floating away from the one in whom my being was complete. I remember this earlier time before I even arrived in my mother's womb. And I was perfectly happy. I couldn't exactly describe to you where I was as I experienced this first call to leave but wherever I was, it was entirely good. And I was not alone. I wanted the 'we', the sweetness of 'we' to last forever. I did not want to become 'I'. But I had to give way to a new power that was shaping me and the forever I knew with that other was lost.

I understand now that it was a gift - I was being offered the gift of life on earth. But I don't think I've ever fully recovered from that first leaving. In darker moments throughout my life, I am sure I hear, ever so faintly, the sorrowful echoes of those wordless times.

Chapter Three

Growing Up

The front door of my childhood home in the small country town of Cowell, in upper Eyre Peninsula, in the state of South Australia, had a wire screen door. Looking out through it one night when the moon hung low enough in the northern sky but high enough to be visible over the neighbour's roof top, I saw light radiating out from the moon. This light spread out in four directions like a cross, like the four points of the body of Jesus on the cross, head, feet and both extended arms. In that moment, I thought I was being blessed with a vision. I had read the stories about the saints with their visions and voices and visitations. I knew it could happen and here, standing in the hallway of my childhood home, I thought I was being blessed with a vision too. I prayed the Rosary every night. I knew Mary, the mother of God had visited children at Fatima;[1] maybe I was being blessed with a sacred vision too?

But that breathless moment didn't last long. As soon as I opened the screen door to go outside, the sacred vision disappeared and the moon became just an ordinary moon and I became just an ordinary little girl. It was the cross-hatching of the wire door that had created the halo effect. I was about ten years old at the time, still young enough to be

---

1. Mary appeared on six occasions to three young children near the village of Fatima in Portugal in 1917. Her message centered on a call for the world to turn away from sin in order to pray for peace.

sure that such miraculous things could happen. But my personal journey into the Divine didn't start there.

Thanks to the faith of my parents and my grandparents on both sides of my family and all my earlier ancestors who kept the faith, handing it down to each generation, God has never been a stranger to me. I think this makes me one of the lucky ones. I did not grow up thinking the idea of God was absurd. I was brought up from birth surrounded by the knowledge of the Divine. In my Catholic home, I knew there was God the Father and Jesus the Son and there was Mary the mother of Jesus and there were countless angels and saints whose stories I heard and read about once I was old enough to read. I believed I had a guardian angel all to myself who would 'watch and guard and rule and guide' over my life. I don't remember much about the Holy Spirit, *"the spirit of truth"* who Jesus refers to in John 14:17. Even though the Holy Spirit is mentioned twice in the Apostle's Creed, a prayer which I learnt to pray as a child, my awareness of God was as Father and Son. However, much later in my life, my faith was to come alive through the amazing power of the Holy Spirit, the third person of the Trinity.

There was never a question in my mind about the authenticity of these invisible Gods and saints, heroes and heroines and that they were all available to me at any moment. I only had to ask. I loved reading about how so many of these 'saints' were committed to helping the poor and the needy. They seemed to demonstrate the love of Jesus in their lives in ways that were truly inspiring.

We were brought up attending Mass, the main formal Catholic church service. Mass is a strange word to use when referring to a worship service. The term is a hangover from the official language of Latin which was used worldwide in the Catholic Church for worship services until only a few decades ago. It comes from the Latin phrase used at the end of the service to dismiss the congregation: *Ite, missa est.* The literal meaning is: *Go, it or she (you or the church) is sent,* as in sent out into the world to preach the good news. But the simple English translation used today is: *Go, the mass has ended.* The Mass is a beautifully choreographed formal service offered daily in remembrance of Jesus' sacrifice on the cross. Like many other Christian services, it includes formal prayers, scripture readings, the communion meal and on Sundays, you might hear music, singing and a sermon.

Growing up as I did in regional South Australia, where the parish priest had to cover several towns across hundreds of miles, meant that my family didn't attend Mass very often. Sometimes the priest would only get to our town fortnightly or even monthly. However, I learnt more about the life of Jesus from the prayer of the Rosary that our family prayed together every night than I ever did from my irregular church attendance. The Rosary is not mentioned as such in the scriptures although it does include the Our Father which Jesus taught us to pray (Matthew 6) and also some of the words Elizabeth, Mary's cousin spoke to her. (Luke 1:42).

The Rosary is a formal prayer that emerged in the Middle Ages. It is not, as some claim, a way of elevating Mary above Jesus. It is a prayer that honours Mary for the unique role she agreed to in God's Divine redemptive plan, that of the mother of Jesus.[2] In the Rosary, we approach Mary as an intercessor, someone who can pray for us. As people pray these prayers in the established pattern, they are encouraged to reflect prayerfully on key moments in the life of Jesus. Before meditation became popular in the secular world, Catholics had their own meditative prayer practice. I may not have been taught to read the Bible as a child but I remain grateful for the role the Rosary played in building my faith in the Jesus story. I can't say I always entered into that prayer in the right spirit but I believe that this daily prayer practice sustained over the first sixteen years of my life, focussing me as it did, on the key events and messages of Jesus' life, built spiritual foundations that God has been able to build upon.

The short version of the Rosary takes about 15-20 minutes, and, in our family, there was no getting away from it. After the evening meal, we would go into the lounge room and kneel around the room to pray the Rosary out loud together. Well, our mother and whatever children were still living at home knelt, but our father walked up and down whilst praying. I never questioned why he gave himself permission to walk whilst we all knelt, it was just how we did things in our home. I always chose to kneel near a corner armchair because that way I could at least distract myself by gazing at the covers of magazines that lay in the corner tables. And it ensured I looked away from the discomforting view of the painting that hung above the piano. In this picture, Jesus was inviting the rich young man to leave all behind him and come follow him (Matthew 19:16-22). It seemed a terrible choice to me. Was there no in between path? Couldn't I have God and a little bit of riches? Dietrich Bonhoeffer's answer to this question is hard to hear. Bonhoeffer, a German theologian, who truly lived out his message about 'costly grace,' was killed by

---

2. There are many Catholic teachings about Mary that I no longer subscribe to. I honour Mary as the mother of Jesus and often ask her to pray for me in the same way I ask my friends to pray for me.

the Nazis just before the end of WWII. The problem for modern Christians, he writes, is that we have been seduced by 'cheap grace'.[3] Cheap grace, he says, is being willing to accept all the grace God offers us through Jesus whilst holding ourselves back, refusing to submit our lives to full discipleship and obedience. In this teaching, Bonhoeffer refers to the parable of the rich young man. A rich young man tells Jesus he has obeyed all the laws and commandments and is now ready for more. *"What do I still lack?"* he asks. Jesus responds with this invitation *"If you want to be perfect……. Go sell your possessions and give to the poor … then come and follow me"* Matthew 19:21.

Money is important and having enough of it to live with dignity is important. Countless institutions and charitable services both locally and across the world are supported through the generosity of large and small donors. That support has to come from somewhere. How many country towns across Australia benefit from the generosity of local businesses, local benefactors? I have been the beneficiary of such generosity.

From the many scriptural exhortations to give generously, *"for God loves a cheerful giver"* 2 Corinthians 9:6-8, it seems that the problem with earthly riches lies more in the attitude of our hearts to it, what we do with it and how attached we are to it.

As Paul says in Philippians 4:12-13, *"For I have learned to be content whatever the circumstances. I know what it is to be in need, and I know what it is to have plenty. I have learned the secret of being content in any and every situation, whether well fed or hungry, whether living in plenty or in want. I can do everything through him who gives me strength."*

I still remain confronted by Jesus' invitation, *"then come and follow me."* God's call is there for all of us. How do we respond? With a full heart or do we bargain with God? Am I truly listening to the call? To what degree are my ears blocked by my love of what the world offers?

Back to the sweet prayer of the Rosary. Even in summer when we went to the beach after school - loaded into the car with our evening dinner of sandwiches and cake or biscuits, we prayed in the car coming home. I remember willingly volunteering to open the gates along the road home that were always closed to keep sheep in various paddocks, because

---

3. (Bonhoeffer, 2018) Ch 1

it meant I would at least miss out on a few Hail Marys. Or if we were lucky, we would catch a ride home in our friend's car and they were not Catholic so no Rosary at all!

Given this environment, I quite naturally continued to grow in my understanding and practice of the basic rituals and prayers of the Catholic Church. And so, at the appropriate age of around seven or eight, I made my first confession.

Since the Catholic community in Cowell was not wealthy enough to have its own church, an array of community spaces were hired for services, including The Country Women's Association (CWA) Hall and the supper room behind the local Institute. There were no private confessionals in these spaces, so I learnt how to confess my sins kneeling next to the priest whilst he sat on a normal chair.[4]

I'm not sure about what I ever said during confession. Maybe I had been unkind to one of my sisters or to a classmate or maybe I had had unkind thoughts, but for several years I hid a true sin that bothered me. I had stolen money. I know now that there is no hierarchy where sin is concerned. Before God all sins are equal. But at that time, stealing money seemed like a real sin to me. I had taken threepence from my Grade Two classroom. Somehow, I had discovered that the teacher kept a jar of loose coins in the back cupboard in the classroom. One day I took a silver threepence from that jar and hid it in the trunk of a tree in the playground and then made a big noise about suddenly discovering it. As I predicted, finding it out there in the playground, it became mine. I have no idea what I spent that huge amount of money on but it did bring me years of guilt and shame. I was in Grade Seven before I could bring myself to confess that sin, I was so ashamed of myself.

On only one other occasion did I ever steal. I'd been sent by my mother down to buy bread from the baker's shop. I think it was unusual to go anywhere by myself and so I must have taken advantage of that and I bought something else with the spare change. I don't remember what I bought but I made sure I finished it before I got home. My mother knew of course because on my return with the loaf of bread I didn't have enough change. I don't remember how she punished me; probably her questioning me about the missing money and her subsequent disappointed disapproving look was enough. I never stole again - ever.

---

4. I didn't know then that there is no need to ask forgiveness for sins from anyone but God. 1 John 1:9

I was eight years old when I received communion for the first time. This was the next major step in my developing faith life as a young Catholic. I still have my framed certificate from that day. It shows Jesus surrounded by his disciples, celebrating that fateful last supper, the first communion meal, before he was dragged away by the authorities and hung on a cross to die.

Throughout the many centuries since that night, debates have raged about whether the communion meal is really the flesh and blood of Jesus Christ as Jesus claims.

"While they were eating, Jesus took bread, gave thanks and broke it, and gave it to his disciples, saying, 'Take and eat; this is my body'. Then he took the cup, gave thanks and offered it to them, saying, 'Drink from it, all of you. This is my blood of the covenant, which is poured out for many for the forgiveness of sins'" Matthew 26:26-27.

Catholics believe that during Mass, the bread and wine do become the body and blood of Jesus. Other Christian churches believe the bread and wine *represent* the body and blood of Jesus. Understanding around the communion meal remains a point of difference between the many Christian churches that have proliferated since the time of the Reformation. Fortunately, those of us who profess belief in a literal interpretation of this teaching, are no longer killed because of it!

Let's go back to my first communion when I was finally going to be old enough to partake of this controversial meal. Although Jesus Christ, King of Kings and Lord of Lords was born in a humble stable, such a sacred ritual apparently couldn't take place in the tiny Cowell, Country Women's Association (CWA) hall. We had to drive a hundred miles or so to a real church, the Port Lincoln church, St Mary of the Angels. That was a long way back then. So early on Sunday morning 17th January 1960, my twin sister and I, 8-year-olds, and probably some of our other older sisters who still lived at home, were woken up early and loaded into the butter yellow Zephyr in our glorious white first communion dresses. I remember we had to stop along the way, perhaps I felt car sick which was not uncommon for me or perhaps someone had to take a toilet break in the bushes. Any way we made it to the church in time. I don't remember having any especially holy or sacred insights during this special day. In fact the only thing I remember clearly was the jelly served up for dessert at the celebratory lunch that followed the church service.

As I have said, I'm no theologian but I have my own story to tell around this meal. Long after my first communion, I was to be gifted with an experience that has verified for me the power of this amazing meal. I will write more about that in a later chapter.

In early high school, I was 'confirmed' into my Catholic faith. As the word suggests, confirmation invites a believer to publicly confirm their faith and beliefs. Given most Catholics are baptised as babies, and so don't get to make that fully informed faith decision at our baptism, confirmation provides this opportunity. Confirmation also purports to strengthen believers in their faith walk by conferring on them the gifts of the Holy Spirit. I'm all in favour of the seven gifts as outlined in Isaiah 11:2-3 that are referred to in the Catholic confirmation ritual: wisdom, understanding, knowledge, fortitude, counsel, piety and fear of the Lord. But the New Testament scriptures talk about another set of amazing gifts from the Holy Spirit, gifts that enable us to live an empowered life with: words of wisdom, words of knowledge, faith, gifts of healing, miraculous powers, prophecy, distinguishing of spirits, various kinds of tongues and interpretation of tongues. I mean this is another set of gifts entirely. However, sadly they were not the gifts I was taught about in preparation for my confirmation.

Given all that scripture says about the Holy Spirit, at my confirmation, I should have fallen under this almighty power. I should have arisen a changed person, alive to God in new and empowering ways but nothing changed for me - no secret switch was turned on. It was to be many years before the power of the Holy Spirit fell on me and changed my life forever.

I listened carefully to the words spoken at a recent confirmation ceremony I attended. It took place in a most beautiful sacred space, and I looked around for you Jesus. Where are you, I asked? You must be here somewhere? This is your house; these words are talking about you and your spirit? The words being uttered were indeed beautiful and powerful; why weren't the children swooning? Why weren't they crying out in delight at your coming? Why weren't they breaking out in tongues? But all I could see was you, Jesus, naked and bound in a back corner behind the altar. Naked, bound and gagged. Such a shocking image. I looked again at the circle of innocent children and their adoring attentive parents sitting in the front pews of the cavernous church. It was clear no one else was seeing what I saw, the bound and gagged Jesus. It crossed my mind to stand up and cry out and draw attention to him - but of course I didn't.

I understand that faith is more than a feeling. *"Now faith is being sure of what we hope for and certain of what we do not see" Hebrews 11:1.* However, although I progressed through the sacramental steps following the normal schedule for young Catholics, I felt no different after any of these sacred liturgical ceremonies: not confession; not communion and not confirmation.

As for baptism - well I had been baptised as a baby, something Catholics do, it seems to me, with no scriptural backing. What a clever trick of the father of lies, Satan, to slip infant baptism into the early church, thereby robbing people of this most important decision. Although I believe baptism is important – no baby sprinkled in baptism is saved by it. Faith in what Jesus accomplished on the cross saves us.[5]

"For it is by grace you have been saved, through faith- and this not from yourselves, it is the gift of God- not by works, so that no one can boast" Ephesians 2:8-9.

Baptism is an outward sign we take to publicly declare what has already occurred in our heart. Because my baptism as a baby had involved no such personal thought or choice, I chose to get baptised again as an adult. It saddens me to say that if I'd done that during the middle ages, that is if I had chosen to publicly acknowledge my personal faith in Jesus Christ as an adult by getting baptised a second time, I would have been reported to the Church hierarchy, handed over to local Inquisitors, those willing torturers sanctioned by decree of the popes of their day and killed. Known as Anabaptists, tens of thousands of those who supported adult baptism were slaughtered during the Catholic Inquisition.

Although I am grateful to my parents for bringing me up to believe in God, I did not experience the life changing love or power of God during my time in the Catholic Church. I did not meet the Jesus I know today. I acknowledge that others may have different experiences. The Catholic catechism explicitly teaches that spiritual progress will lead to greater intimacy with God – even to a 'mystical' union. The Catholic Church has a long history of mystics, holy men and women who did (and no doubt still do) develop deep and personal relationships with God. But that was not my experience. I understood that as long as I complied occasionally with Church rituals and traditions, and lived a fairly good life, I would go to heaven when I died. I don't remember being taught that salvation

---

5. Some Protestant churches still adhere to the practice of infant baptism even though during the Reformation they rejected many other non-scriptural practices of the Catholic Church.

was a gift. I repeat this important scripture: *"For it is by grace you have been saved through faith – and this is not from yourselves, it is the gift of God – not by works, so that no one can boast"* Ephesians 2:8-9.

What I didn't yet know was that salvation and following church traditions and rituals were not the same thing. I could not earn my way into Heaven. I had much to learn.

Stepping Stones 1

- Finished 5 years as a boarder at a Catholic high school in Adelaide
- Completed 5 years at university and teachers' college in Adelaide
- Graduated with a Diploma in Teaching and a Bachelor of Arts degree (Honours)
- Posted as a secondary school English and History teacher to Ceduna, the last major South Australian town on the highway heading to Western Australia

Chapter Four

Hungry for More

I lived a conservative, timid life during my university and teacher's college years. Even after five years of student life, I had only a very small circle of friends and acquaintances. Then I doubled down on my lonely tendencies and applied for a teaching position in Ceduna, a town that was almost the farthest western outpost in South Australia. I knew no one there.

I had no idea what to expect having never been there even though my oldest three siblings had been born there. The contract I'd entered into with the Education Department to get paid to train as a teacher meant that upon graduation, I had to spend my first two years teaching in a country setting.

Without easy access to any siblings and without the skills of building friendships very successfully and without a church community to turn to, I was very alone. Since leaving the enforced liturgical events of boarding school life, I had rejected most of the rituals of Catholicism. God was no longer a significant part of my life even though I still identified publicly as a Catholic.

I decided to begin my new post-student life, by reinvigorating my spiritual life. Would I have felt this hunger for God if I'd been busy and happily socialising with an established close circle of friends and family? Would I have sought God if I'd managed to fall in and out of love as regularly as so many of my teaching colleagues seemed to be capable of? I will never know the answers to these questions but I see now that the isolation I experienced on my arrival in this remote far western town, did me a great service, it pushed me to find God.

The first thing I decided to do was to start going to Mass again. It didn't occur to me that there may have been other paths to finding God. I didn't yet know enough about the nature of God to understand that this Divine creator is accessible anytime, anywhere, anyplace and so I went back to the only church I knew. The Catholic Church in Ceduna sat lonely on a rise about halfway between the town of Ceduna and the port of Thevenard. It looked out over the sheltered waters of Murat Bay which glittered and sparkled in the forever sunshine of Ceduna. But my weak faith was not inspired or strengthened by my attendance at church services. On the contrary, the sparkling waters of the bay spoke more powerfully to me of the nature of God and so it wasn't long before I swapped church on Sundays for sailing and other outdoor activities. I reasoned that if God was to be found, I could do that more easily out in the beauty of the natural world.

Along with the practical matters of learning to become a teacher, Ceduna as a location proved to be a very happy and helpful time for me. The beauty of Murat Bay on a calm day was something to behold and the surrounding coastline was magnificent. I finally emerged into a sunny, less lonely life. During my years of teacher training, I had hated every session of practice teaching that I'd had to complete but to my surprise, I discovered I liked teaching. I enjoyed the fun and energy of my teaching colleagues. I loved the privilege of engaging meaningfully with students. Surfing and fishing and farming were the dominant cultures. At that time Ceduna was in many ways a frontier town, and so it attracted its share of wanderers. I loved my life, and for the very first time I felt it was my life I was living. It was a healthy time in many ways but God was still an elusive concept.

My teaching contract stipulated I had to serve two years at a country school. I began to think about what I would do after that. Perhaps I would travel overseas? It was common practice for young people in the mid-70s to take off to Europe after graduation. Some went for an extended holiday; some went intending to work for one or two years, perhaps the beginning of the gap year practice, before returning home to pursue a more serious life. Maybe that's what I needed? So in my second year at Ceduna, I began saving towards that goal.

To avoid landing in London in mid-winter, I applied to stay teaching at Ceduna beyond my compulsory two year bond but just for Term One. However the Education Department thought I could solve another problem they had further down the highway. They had a Term One vacancy 150 kms down the track at Wudinna – would I take it? Quick calculations reassured me Wudinna was close enough for me to travel back to Ceduna each weekend for sport and other social commitments. Another term's work would also enable me to save a bit more money for this supposed adventure of a lifetime. I accepted. Little did I know that I would find something far more radical and life changing in Wudinna than an overseas trip could deliver.

Even though by the end of my two years in Ceduna, I'd dropped any pretence of going to Mass, I had not rejected God totally. I was still open and listening and searching. Although I wasn't mixing with the local Catholic community, I knew from other family members that interesting things were happening across Christian churches. The charismatic renewal which had officially emerged in the US towards the end of the 1960's was spreading around the world and by the mid-1970s, just as I was trying to work out my future and my faith life, it had taken root in major cities in Australia. Whilst this new movement had begun in Protestant churches, by the mid-1970s Catholics alike were picking up on the teachings surrounding this movement. Baptism of the Holy Spirit began to be spoken of. The Ecumenical movement was also taking off. Christian churches of various persuasions began to focus more on what they had in common rather than on divisions of the past.

The Charismatic renewal was about relating to God in new ways. This new experience of God began once someone was baptised in the Holy Spirit. This was something quite different from water baptism. It was the modern equivalent of the Pentecost day that Paul writes about in Acts 2, when tongues of fire descended on the disciples and the crowds who had gathered and they burst out speaking in tongues and manifesting other 'charisms' or sacred gifts. Once you were ready to be baptised in the Holy Spirit other members of the Christian community would pray for this by laying their hands on your head or shoulders and asking for the Holy Spirit to come. It was essentially as simple as this and yet life changing. Speaking in tongues, a gift available to all, would then follow along with other sacred gifts such as prophesying or delivering words of knowledge and wisdom. All of these supernatural gifts became part of charismatic communal worship sessions.

I had heard about all of this from my brother and sister-in-law. I trusted them completely and so I determined to find out more. During my summer holidays before I returned to the Eyre Peninsula for what I thought would be my last term of teaching prior to heading off to London, I did some research. I was curious enough about this new movement to find a Catholic charismatic meeting in Adelaide that I could attend. I sat somewhere in the back row of seats in a hall embarrassed to be there amidst such overt conviviality and robust singing! I'd never heard singing like that in a religious setting before. I was intrigued. Even though I tried to make myself invisible in the back of the hall, the room exuded an attractive warmth. I wanted what they had.

As with everything with which we humans are involved, there is some debate about the merits of the charismatic movement. Has it strengthened or weakened the church? Some say that it encourages believers to focus on emotions and feelings rather than on faith in the Lord Jesus. They say its messages about love and prosperity have replaced a focus on the costs of true discipleship. I remain grateful that it helped me find God.

But I was heading to London and so I returned to Wudinna to take up what I thought would be my final term of teaching.

Chapter Five

Finding God in Kyancutta

Wudinna was and still is, a small town. When I arrived in 1976, there were about seven hundred people living in the township itself and perhaps one thousand in the surrounding districts. The school population was around two hundred and seventy, ranging from Year 1 through to a small cohort of Year 12 students. With two years' teaching experience under my belt, I felt a little more confident in taking up this post. After all it would only be for one term and then I would be off to London. I had made absolutely no plans about my overseas trip so during the next few months I needed to make decisions about flights and where I would land and what I would actually do when I arrived. Such confidence was not unplaced; I had travelled on my own before. As part of my university studies, I had made all the necessary arrangements to go to Pitcairn Island a remote British outpost in the South Pacific, (of Mutiny on the Bounty fame) to complete research for my History Honours thesis - so of course I believed I could pull this proposed trip to London together, given it was a much more conservative destination.

I settled in well to my teaching life in Wudinna, maintaining my social ties with Ceduna by travelling back each weekend to sail and stay over with friends. I knew my teaching skills had improved since I'd begun in Ceduna two years earlier but I was taking the place of a senior teacher so it was a step up. Even though I was only a temporary replacement, I took my teaching very seriously. We weren't far into Term One when my Wudinna teaching colleagues began to tease me, oh he (the teacher I was replacing) won't be coming back they'd say. You'll need to stay here till the end of the year. They'd laugh, knowing I was intending to travel. I laughed with them but inwardly I was worried. On the surface, Wudinna did not seem to offer much for a 24-year-old single woman.

One evening midterm (at the time it was a three-term school year) so perhaps around Easter, early enough to still be light and warm outside, the headmaster turned up at the front door of the house where I was living. I liked and respected this man. He was truly a gentleman, hardworking and totally engaged with his school community. He asked me would I consider staying on for the rest of the year. The senior teacher whose place I was filling would not be returning. Inside I panicked. Outside I remained calm. I respected the way this man ran his school community and I was proud that he would even want me, a junior teacher, to become a permanent member of his team. He asked me to consider it and to give him an answer soon.

The memory of the next few moments remain with me indelibly. I said I would consider his request and closed the screen door and went into my bedroom. I fell on my knees, something I was not accustomed to doing, not since my childhood days of saying the Rosary. I cried out to God who, at that time, I didn't really know would be listening. I certainly wasn't expecting to hear an answer. Panicked at the thought of being trapped in this small town, literally in the middle of nowhere, I went down on my knees and said to God. *"I'll go anywhere,* (suddenly London didn't seem to matter) *I'll go to India - just get me out of Wudinna."* Remember, I was twenty four years old at the time, single (despite falling desperately in love with a dreamy piano player in Ceduna and he barely noticing me) and had no partnership prospects in sight. What could another remote small town in regional Australia offer me! This is what I heard:

You can't go to India but you can stay in Wudinna.

I was not quite aware at the time where this message had come from but the power of it reduced me to immediate tears! Later, I identified this message as my first message from God, a breakthrough action of a God I had not yet come to know much about. But God or not, after the outburst of tears, I went straight into bargaining mode. But if I stay here, I won't find you God. I have to be in a town big enough to have a charismatic prayer group! I was by then convinced this would be the way I would find this elusive God. Since I knew there wasn't a charismatic prayer group in Wudinna, it was clear to me that I would have to leave Wudinna. Any sensible God wanting to be found would understand this and help me relocate.

However never underestimate God! Just a few days later, as I was reading the local paper, I saw a small two or three-line advertisement in the classified ads at the back of the paper. It was an open invitation to attend a charismatic prayer group hosted by local members of the Methodist Church (later to become the Uniting Church). I was stunned. Had I not bargained with God just a few days earlier to get me out of Wudinna so I could attend just such a prayer group, so I could learn more about God? Was this a direct answer? I could stay in Wudinna and here was the charismatic renewal on my doorstep. True it wasn't with the Catholics but that didn't worry me too much. I was amazed and overwhelmed by this coincidence. On the basis of that startling intervention, I told the Headmaster I would stay. And as it turned out I stayed for four more years!

The newspaper advertisement was for a Saturday evening meeting to be held at the Kyancutta General Store. Kyancutta is a railway siding, about 13 kms south of Wudinna. At that time, Kyancutta consisted of silos, a railway siding and a General Store with petrol pumps and not much else. If I feared Wudinna was a small town, then Kyancutta was even less significant! I rang the number that was in the advertisement just to check I had the date, the time and the place right. I didn't give my name. I felt too embarrassed and shy to do that. And it was always possible I might pull out at the last minute! On the following Saturday evening, I hopped on my Honda 250 XL trail bike, then my only mode of transport, and headed south. I entered a large lounge room where a circle of perhaps five or six couples were already seated, people whom I came to love and appreciate very dearly over the next few years. I was invited to take a seat. The theme of the evening was to seek God's direction for the group. How should they proceed as a prayer group? What direction should they take? My presence would have been a surprise. They would have known I was a new teacher, but I hadn't met any of them before that night. Whilst they were praying with their eyes shut, I opened my eyes and looked around. I can clearly remember my overriding impression that evening was that these people were talking to a God who they seemed to believe was actually real, who was present and listening to their conversations, their discussions and their prayerful and humble requests.

As I rode back that evening on my bike, I felt a new sense of jubilation and direction. I couldn't explain with words what had happened. I just knew something significant had happened. I was excited to know more about this God who could reach through the veil into my world to meet me in such an individual and personalised way, finding me a charismatic prayer group in the middle of Eyre Peninsula. Me, the lapsed Catholic had been introduced to the living God in the midst of Protestants. My life changed that night. Without a doubt. God may have known and loved me from the beginning of time but that night in Kyancutta, I found God and my life was changed forever.

It's not that I was given new theological knowledge. It wasn't that this group of people had persuaded me with clever arguments or debates. I had encountered a new dimension that impacted me somewhere other than my mind. My emotions were engaged, my soul, my spirit had been gently touched. I left that meeting with a light sense of joy and impending excitement. I felt I was visible in a way I'd never been before, visible to some almighty loving presence. I had found something, someone, perhaps even God. I was no longer searching or lost.

I am so grateful to that group of believers. I owe them a huge debt of gratitude for their obedience in meeting together to seek the will of God for their lives. I don't think I ever thanked them enough for the courage they showed in being early adopters of the wave of renewal that was sweeping across the Christian church during the 1960's and 1970's. They took me, a raw unschooled recruit, into the Kingdom of God right there in remote country South Australia. I was led to springs of living water – how blessed I was.

And even more surprising to me who was such an unschooled novice in spiritual matters, I developed a hunger to read the Bible. I had never read one before so I didn't own one. However thanks to the Gideons, that amazing organisation that leaves Bibles in public places, most notably hotels, I found a small New Testament sitting in the magazine racks in the Wudinna Area School staff room. I took it home with me to read and was surprised to find how directly it could speak to me about what was happening in my life. Without realising it at the time, I had discovered the awesome power of the Word of God.

A Few Words About Jesus

He is the image of the invisible God, the firstborn over all creation. For by him all things were created: things in heaven and on earth, visible and invisible, whether thrones or power or rulers or authorities; all things were created by him and for him. He is before all things, and in him all things hold together.

Colossians 1:15-17

"Do not let your hearts be troubled. Trust in God, trust also in me. In my Father's house are many rooms; if it were not so, I would have told you. I'm going there to prepare a place for you. And if I go and prepare a place for you, I will come back and take you to be with me that you also may be where I am. You know the way to the place where I am going."

Thomas said to him, 'Lord we don't know where you are going, so how can we know the way?' Jesus answered, 'I am the way and the truth and the life. No one comes to the Father except through me.'"

John 14:1-6

Chapter Six

More About Jesus

Ecclesiastes is a short book in the Old Testament, thought to be written by King Solomon. In a chapter titled, "Stand in awe of God," I find this instruction:

"God is in Heaven, and you are on earth. So let your words be few" Ecclesiastes 5:2.

Despite this injunction, before I get back into my story about the early lessons God taught me, I want to say a few direct words about this amazing man-God, Jesus; just enough, I hope, to send you on your own journey towards him.

"Beyond all question, the mystery of godliness is great:

He appeared in a body, was vindicated by the Spirit, was seen by angels, was preached among the nations, was believed on in the world, was taken up in glory" 1 Timothy 3:16.

Jesus was no normal man. His arrival on earth had been prophesied about in detail for many centuries before he arrived. There are over one hundred references about the coming of this Saviour in the Old Testament. What other religious/spiritual leader can claim that? Some examples of these prophecies are:

"For unto us a child is born ...... and he will be called Wonderful Counsellor, Mighty God, Everlasting Father, Prince of Peace. Of the increase of his government and peace there will be no end" Isaiah 9:6.

Even in the early days after the week of creation, when Adam and Eve were still in the garden, God warned Satan that although he may have succeeded in deceiving our first parents and consequently leading the whole human race astray, he wouldn't win in the end. God was going to send someone who would ultimately defeat Satan, the father of lies.

"And I will put enmity between you and the woman, and between your offspring and hers; he will crush your head, and you will bruise his heel" Genesis 3:15.

This Saviour was going to be born of a virgin. *"Therefore the Lord himself will give you a sign. The virgin will be with child and will give birth to a son and will call him Immanuel"* (Immanuel means 'God is with us') *Isaiah 7:14.*

He was going to be born in Bethlehem, an unlikely unimportant small town in Judah.

"But you Bethlehem Ephrathah, though you are small among the clans of Judah, out of you will come for me one who will be ruler over Israel whose origins are from of old, from ancient times" Micah 5:2.

His life purpose was to be an offering for our sins, *"the Lord makes his life a guilt offering" Isaiah 53:10*. *"He was pierced for our transgressions" 53:5.* In fact, read all of Isaiah 53, it even includes a physical description of the man Jesus (Isaiah 53:2).

How he was going to be killed was prophesied with eerie detail.

"They have pierced my hands and my feet. I can count all my bones; people stare and gloat over me. They divided my garments amongst them and cast lots for my clothing" Psalm 22:16-18. Read Luke 23 and you will see that the Roman soldiers did all the above to Jesus as he was dying on the cross.

How could this be? How could these amazing details be foretold? Who else but an all-knowing, all-powerful God who sits outside of time could have planted these messages throughout the Old Testament as a way of preparing the Jewish people for the arrival of their Messiah.

Jesus himself knew ahead of time that he was going to die painfully and on at least three occasions he tried to warn his disciples about this. At one stage Jesus drew his twelve disciples aside from the crowds and tells them:

"We are going up to Jerusalem and everything that is written by the prophets about the Son of Man will be fulfilled. He will be handed over to the Gentiles. They will mock him, insult him, spit on him, flog him and kill him. On the third day he will rise again." But as Luke records, *"The disciples did not understand any of this. Its meaning was hidden from them, and they did not know what he was talking about"* Luke 18:31-34.

Let's return our focus to the person of Jesus. Jesus, Son of Mary, stepson of Joseph, Son of God, Saviour, Lord, Redeemer, King of Kings but also fully a man, is one of us with the full range of emotions and challenges that come with being human. Except – that he is without sin! (2 Corinthians 5:21).

"He committed no sin and no deceit was found in his mouth" 1 Peter 2:22.

He was a teacher. Read the Gospels and listen to the stories he told his followers, simple stories that clarified the dense and complicated religious laws of the day, to reveal the loving heart of God and his purposes towards mankind.

He had friends. He calls us friends. (John 15:15). He wept over them. He shared meals with them. He taught them how to pray. He revealed truth to them.

He withdrew from the crowds to seek his Father's face in prayer. He fasted. He wrestled with the devil. Satan is real and so are the hordes of demons (fallen angels) who do his bidding across our world. He cast out these demons from afflicted people.

He introduced us to his Father, our Father too. He had absolute confidence in the provision of his Father, our Father too. He didn't worry about what food he was to eat or where he was going to sleep at night. He always pointed his followers back to having faith in God the Father, our Father.

He taught us how to pray: *"This then, is how you should pray: Our Father in heaven, hallowed be your name" Matthew 6:9* (hallowed means greatly revered and honoured).

He changed water into wine.

He healed the sick. He raised the dead - more than once!

He changed the weather, rebuking the wind and the waves.

He multiplied food supplies twice. Taking a few loaves and dried fishes he fed five thousand and then later fed four thousand, big crowds in those times. These crowds had been mesmerized by Jesus' teachings and his signs and wonders. They had followed him out into the countryside to hear him preach.

He forgave people for their sins; that really got him into trouble.

He told his followers not to worry or be anxious about anything but to keep their eyes fixed on eternal things.

The voice of God spoke out from the Heavens twice over Jesus during the three years of his public ministry. Firstly at his baptism:

"As soon as Jesus was baptised, he went up out of the water. At that moment heaven was opened, and he saw the Spirit of God descending like a dove and lighting on him. And a voice from heaven said, 'this is my Son whom I love; With him I am well pleased'" Matthew 3:16-17.

And three years later just before Jesus' death, this same voice thundered out over those who had come to celebrate the Passover in Jerusalem. Jesus had been speaking to the crowd. He ended by saying:

"Father glorify your name.

Then a voice came from heaven, 'I have glorified it and will glorify it again'. The crowd that was there and heard it, said it had thundered; others said an Angel had spoken to him" John 12:28.

He allowed himself to be killed, not just instantly as with a sword but by crucifixion, considered the most painful form of punishment ever invented by humans. He could have stopped that.

After this slow and painful death, he rose from the dead and was seen by many of his close followers over a period of forty days. During this time he *"gave many convincing proofs that he was alive" Acts 1:3.*

After his resurrection from the dead, he instructed his disciples to wait in Jerusalem,

"...wait for the gift my Father promised ..... For John baptised with water but in a few days, you will be baptised with the Holy Spirit" Acts 1:4-5.

Jesus didn't come to overthrow the political order of the day. However he was radical in other ways, upsetting religious leaders with his interpretation of how religious laws should work and with his messages about the true loving nature of God whom he called Father. His teachings tipped everything on its head.

"Blessed are the poor in spirit, for theirs is the Kingdom of heaven,

Blessed are those who mourn, for they will be comforted.

Blessed are the meek for they will inherit the earth" Matthew 5:3-5.

So how will you know when you belong to God? Is there a path, signposts, a gate, a strategy? How will you know if you've passed from mere curiosity and research into the Kingdom of God itself? Will you know when you've arrived. Will you know when you've been saved?

The New Testament is full of instructions about this:

"If we confess our sins, he is faithful and just and will forgive us our sins and purify us from all unrighteousness" 1 John 1:9.

"That if you confess with your mouth, 'Jesus is Lord,' and believe in your heart that God raised him from the dead, you will be saved" Romans 10:9.

The concept of sin may be challenging to some. We might think we are pretty good citizens of the world doing our best to help others and going about our business quietly and without drama. However, at our core we want to do things our way, not God's way. That's sin right there!

Once when Paul and Silas were in prison for preaching the gospel, God caused an earthquake which resulted in all the prison doors flying open and all prisoners' chains coming loose. The guard was so worried that he would be blamed for freeing the prisoners, he drew his sword and was about to kill himself until Paul shouted at him: *"Don't harm yourself! We are all here."* The jailer was so overcome that he fell trembling before Paul and asked: *"What must I do to be saved?"* And Paul and Silas answered him *"Believe in the*

Lord Jesus and you will be saved – you and your household" Acts 16:25-31. Giving your life to Jesus can be as simple as that.

Peter preached to the crowd in Jerusalem on the day the Holy Spirit fell on Jesus followers just as he had promised. He set out before them how they had been complicit in killing their promised Messiah. Ashamed, they asked Peter what they should do. Peter said to them:

"Repent and be baptised, every one of you, in the name of Jesus Christ for the forgiveness of your sins..." Acts 2:38.

Many of today's churches share their beliefs online, outlining how to become a Christian. Some are easier to follow than others. I prefer the faith summaries found on the websites of Pentecostal churches because they are not shy about promoting the baptism of the Holy Spirit. Pentecostal Churches take their name from the Greek word *pentecostē*, which means "fiftieth day". This special holy day of Pentecost is celebrated in all Christian churches on the first Sunday that comes fifty days after Easter. This was when the Holy Spirit first descended in tongues of fire on the heads of Jesus' followers as he promised would happen after his ascension into heaven (Acts 2).

A typical summary of steps to becoming a Christian will include something like this: believe in Jesus, repent of your sins, accept Jesus paid the price for your sins through his death on the cross, thank Jesus and commit to obeying his teachings and following him, be baptised in water, be baptised in the Holy Spirit, and receive whatever gifts the Holy Spirit wants to offer you.

Everyone can receive the gift of speaking in tongues. Don't feel awkward about that, just open your mouth and let new sounds come out. But there are other gifts too: words of knowledge, prophecy, and healing. Be open to all that God has in store for you. Start living your new life guided by the power of the Holy Spirit, the comforter, the gift of our Father, the one who will lead us in spirit and in truth. And if you do go looking for a Christian community, choose one that openly promotes the baptism of the Holy Spirit.

The Holy Spirit is the unsung hero of my story. Jesus is Lord and Saviour. Jesus introduces us to the Father. Then, as he prepared to leave the earth, he gave us the Holy Spirit, our helper, counsellor, and guide. Through this humble third person of the Trinity, we are given unlimited access to God – at no cost. The Holy internet of the Trinity – paid for in full by Jesus! As if that isn't enough, the Holy Spirit brings further gifts to empower us to live the life God wants us to. All offered freely – come, come and receive. Open your hearts and your minds.

I want people who read my story to not only meet Jesus but I also want them to receive the full power he intended for us to have. We are shortchanged without the Holy Spirit being fully released in our lives.

But even though I have described above the steps you could take to become a follower of Jesus, everyone's story is different. The presence of God can fall wordlessly and instantly on a person who is seeking God. I didn't find God following the steps I have just outlined above. As I described in an earlier chapter, I encountered God when I saw the Holy Spirit operating in others around me. I don't remember saying any particular words or prayers. I knew I had met God that night just from sitting for two hours in the company of a group of believers I didn't even know. Two weeks later, I asked to be baptised in the Holy Spirit. It was simple, hands were laid on my shoulders and someone prayed that the Holy Spirit would fall on me. I did not speak in tongues at that time. It felt awkward and I was embarrassed when the promised new language didn't flow out of my mouth immediately. But I was encouraged to go home and get out of the English language and open my mouth with other sounds. And that is indeed what happened and a new language poured out of me. I had never understood till then what it meant to praise God. I was taken up entirely with a new way to honour and praise this amazing God who was showing himself to me.

I didn't know I'd received the gift of prophecy until sometime later, when in the middle of a meeting, my body trembled, my arms tingled and I felt I needed to open my mouth and words came out that I did not compose. And as I've written earlier, I'd already been baptized in water as a child so I didn't immediately ask to be baptised again. But I did several years later. I wanted to choose that outward sign of accepting Jesus as my Lord, as an adult.

We are all unique individuals loved by God and his wooing of us will be tailored to suit whatever our situation may be. You may be in extreme pain, physical or emotional. You may have past hurts that simply won't let you go. You may be caught in addictions. You may have a lifetime of disbelief or outright cynicism. You may just have a space in your being that you can't satisfy. Or you may be simply curious. You may already believe in God but have no power, no personal experience of him. In this case you might just need the power of the Holy Spirit released in your life. Perhaps you are already a Christian. You have been baptised and once walked closely with Jesus but you've lost touch. Life has become too difficult and you've lost that first love. Whatever your situation, when you draw near to God, God, through the power of his Holy Spirit, will draw near to you and you will know. That's just how his love works. Some words I received in my early days:

> *You know I am the Great Lover and I do not say this to you lightly. You know something of the joy of discovering the other, of beginning to love the other. Imagine my joy when I pursue my children, my own in love. How hungry I am for that to be consummated and I love all to the same depth.*

> *....... If you only knew how I long to sit and share myself with you. Always I am waiting. Come to me simply and expectantly, cleansed by my forgiveness, my love.*

> *How often do I show you the way and still you turn away. But I am like the beggar at the gate, I persist, so great is my love for you.*

God wants to meet with us. He wants a relationship. He is the greatest lover on earth and in the heavens! Trust him to get you there. Why not pause right here, right now. If you've never known God then ask Jesus to be your Lord and Saviour. Or if you've lost your way, come back to him. Rededicate yourself to following Jesus. His love and forgiveness is there for all.

Jesus is coming back

On the last day he spent on earth with his disciples, Jesus confirmed his earlier instructions to them about the coming of the Holy Spirit: *"Do not leave Jerusalem but wait for the gift my Father promised......But you will receive power when the Holy Spirit comes on you; and you will be my witnesses in Jerusalem and in all Judea and Samaria and to the ends of the earth" Acts 1:4-8.* And then without any warning, he was bodily taken up into the sky. Two men, dressed in white, (we can assume they were angels) spoke to the startled disciples and told them that Jesus would return to earth in the same way: *"After he said this, he was taken up before their very eyes, and a cloud hid him from their sight. They were looking intently up into the sky as he was going, when suddenly two men dressed in white stood beside them. "Men of Galilee," they said, "why do you stand here looking into the sky? This same Jesus, who has been taken from you into heaven, will come back in the same way you have seen him go into heaven" Acts 1:9-11.*

That's right, Jesus is coming back.

Before his death and ascension into heaven, the disciples came to Jesus and asked him when the time of his return would come. He had just delivered a fierce rebuke to the teachers of the law and to the Pharisees about their hypocrisy. In no uncertain terms, he told them that they did not practise what they preached. Then he ended by saying to them rather enigmatically:

"For I tell you, you will not see me again until you say, 'Blessed is he who comes in the name of the Lord'" Matthew 23:39.

As he left the temple, his disciples drew his attention to the temple buildings and he said to them:

"Do you see all these things?... I tell you the truth, not one stone here will be left on another; everyone will be thrown down" Matthew 24:2.

The disciples asked him what he meant by his words.[1]

"Tell us," they said, "when will this happen, and what will be the sign of your coming and of the end of the age?" Matthew 24:3.

Jesus did not give the disciples a direct answer but rather he replied by describing many of the signs that would indicate that the time of his return would be imminent. His teaching on this is described in great details in Matthew 24. It's an extraordinary chapter. *"Nation will rise against nation and Kingdom against Kingdom. There will be famines*

---

1. Here Jesus was prophesying about the destruction of the temple in Jerusalem well after his death in 70 AD

and earthquakes in various places. All these are the beginning of birth pains" Matthew 24:7-8.

There will be an increase in wickedness across the world, *"great distress, unequalled from the beginning of the world until now- and never to be equalled again" Matthew 24:21. "Immediately after the distress of those days – the sun will be darkened and the moon will not give its light; the stars will fall from the sky, and heavenly bodies will be shaken" Matthew 24:29.*

Jesus also warned the disciples that at this time, false Christs and false prophets will arise who will even perform signs and miracles, trying to deceive believers (Matthew 24:24). But we should not be afraid because it will become clear who the real Jesus is:

And *"At that time the sign of the Son of Man will appear in the sky, and all nations of the earth will mourn. They will see the Son of Man coming on clouds of the sky with power and great glory" Matthew 24:30.*

But no one, not even Jesus himself knows when this day will be. Speaking to his disciples he said this:

"No one knows about that day or hour, not even the angels in heaven nor the Son but only the Father" Matthew 24:36. That's why we should always be ready. *"Therefore keep watch, because you do not know on what day your Lord will come" Matthew 24:42.*

Some biblical scholars believe that Christians living on the earth in the final days, along with unbelievers, will have to endure the seven terrible years of tribulation which the Bible tells us will precede the final great battle of Armageddon. However others believe that Christians living on earth at the end time, will be saved by the Rapture. The word 'Rapture' is not mentioned as such in the Bible but it refers to Christians being 'caught up' as Paul describes in Thessalonians 4:16-17:

"For the Lord himself will come down from heaven, with a loud command, with the voice of the archangel and with the trumpet call of God, and the dead in Christ will rise first. After that, we who are still alive and are left will be caught up together with them in the clouds to meet the Lord in the air. And so we will be with the Lord forever."

What an extraordinary day that will be. All believers who have lived and died throughout history will be the first to rise up to join Jesus in the sky. It's impossible to comprehend the numbers that will fill the skies. And only after the dead have risen will those who happen to be living on earth at this time also be lifted up to meet Jesus in the sky. And this will all happen *"in a flash, in the twinkling of an eye,"* 1 Corinthians 15:52. There will be no warning, no news flash.

Jesus describes the Rapture like this:

"As it was in the days of Noah, so it will be at the coming of the son of man. For in the days before the flood, people were eating and drinking, marrying and giving in marriage, up to the day Noah entered the ark; and they knew nothing about what would happen until the flood came and took them all away. That is how it will be at the coming of the Son of Man. Two men will be in the field; one will be taken and the other left. Two women will be grinding with a hand mill; one will be taken and the other left. Therefore keep watch because you do not know on what day your Lord will come" Matthew 24:37-42.

Believers living on earth at this time will simply disappear. Christian workers will disappear from their workplaces. For those non-believers watching TV or whatever other form of entertainment exists at this time in the future – if one newsreader is a Christian they will disappear and if their cohost is not a believer, they will have no explanation! Consider the disruption this will cause, the mystery of multitudes across the world disappearing from their daily lives with no explanations given. Only those who are familiar with the prophesies about the Rapture might have some idea about what has happened.

Even if, as some Bible teachers tell us, all Christians are taken up into heaven by Jesus at this time, it still won't be too late for unbelievers who are left behind to turn to God. But sadly, those who are left will experience great suffering during the Tribulation. According to prophecy, the coming of the Tribulation will unleash seven years of God's judgement upon the earth. John, in the book of Revelation, describes in terrible detail how the wrath and judgement of God will fall on the earth. It will be a time of unparalleled trials and suffering. Although Dan Ackroyd used the events prophesied in the book of Revelation about these end times to inspire his comic/horror Ghost Buster movies [2], not even the most creative screen writers or film directors could ever imagine what John describes is to come. No one will be able to protect themselves from this time. Only at the end of

---

2. The movies arrived in 1984, 1989, 2016, 2021 and 2024

this time of great suffering and judgement will Jesus return to the earth. This will be his second coming.

The book of Revelation is a challenging read and unusual right from its opening lines where it tells us that what is to follow is a revelation given by God himself to his son Jesus Christ so that Jesus could then show it to his servants, that is to us! Jesus did this by revealing it all to his beloved disciple John, with angels helping. John received this vision in a dream whilst he was living in exile on the island of Patmos. He'd been exiled there by the Roman authorities because of his radical teaching and preaching about Jesus. In the vision, he was instructed to write down everything he saw.

Unlike other parts of the New Testament, the book of Revelation is not about past history. It describes a time in the future; it reveals an apocalypse is coming. The word apocalypse means an event resulting in great destruction and violent change. In Revelation it heralds the complete destruction of the world as we now know it, in order to make way for the new heaven and the new earth that is promised. Although challenging, we are encouraged to read the book of Revelation despite its dark prophetic vision:

"Blessed is the one who reads the words of this prophecy and blessed are those who hear it and take to heart what is written in it," Revelation 1:3.

Ezekiel, prophesying about these end times, nearly 600 years before the birth of Christ, describes with terrible details how this final battle will unfold:

"This is what will happen in that day: when Gog attacks the land of Israel, my hot anger will be aroused, declares the sovereign Lord. In my zeal and fiery wrath I declare that at that time there shall be a great earthquake in the land of Israel" Ezekiel Ch 38:18-19.

Ezekiel goes on to describe more details about what God revealed to him. Mountains will be overturned, plague and bloodshed will abound, hailstones and burning sulphur will rain down on the fighting troops. And then says God:

"And so I will show my greatness and my holiness, and I will make myself known in the sight of many nations. Then they will know that I am the Lord" Ezekiel 38:23.

According to Ezekiel's prophesy, these final battles against the powers of darkness and evil will take place in the land of Israel. The final battle between God and Satan, the one that began at the creation of the world, will play itself out through the geographically small but biblically significant nation of Israel. This is where the feet of Jesus will return to, as the two angels predicted on the day of Jesus' ascension into heaven.

Despite the long-expressed wishes for the total destruction of Israel by many nations surrounding Israel, God is ultimately in control and will deliver on his promise to Abraham, *"all the peoples on earth will be blessed through you."* In the end God will prevail, for the nation of Israel is special to God:

"For you are a people holy to the Lord your God. The Lord your God has chosen you out of all the peoples on the face of the earth to be his people, his treasured possession" Deuteronomy 7:6.

I am not scholarly enough to speak in detail about the role of Israel in the end times but there is much to read and learn that can help us to understand the role this beleaguered nation will play in the end times. Whether we support the politics of the day or not, we should pay close attention to whatever happens in Israel. And we should heed the promise and warning God gave as he proclaimed his covenant with Abraham (then known as Abram):

"I will make you into a great nation and I will bless you; I will make your name great, and you will be a blessing" Genesis 12:2

We should particularly heed the next thing God said:

"I will bless those who bless you, and whoever curses you I will curse; and all peoples on earth will be blessed through you" Genesis 12:3.

At this time of his second coming, Jesus will be revealed in all his power and glory. The fearsome glory and majesty of this is described throughout the book of Revelation. In this book, we see Jesus in a way we've never seen him before, no longer the unassuming, itinerant preacher but a King in all his awesome glory. And what we know, is that when this time comes everyone will know who Jesus really is:

"As surely as I live says the Lord every knee will bow before me; every tongue will confess to God" Romans 14:11.

So don't let your heart grow hard about these matters. God has given us his Word to warn us so that we can prepare ourselves and our families for what lies ahead. Perhaps the things that John writes about in Revelation won't happen in our lifetimes, but we are all going to die sometime and so there is no better time to be prepared than now. To this end, Jesus instructs all of us, in his seven letters to the churches, (Revelation Chapters 2&3), to pay attention to his messages by repeating at the end of each letter:

"He who has an ear, let him hear what the Spirit says to the churches" Revelation 2:7.

John doesn't exactly say it was Jesus talking to him in this vision but from the description of this amazing encounter, it seems clear he was being spoken to by the glorified, transformed, risen Christ. So overwhelmed was John by this vision, that he fell down to the ground as if he was dead. Then this figure, the Son of God himself, reached down and touched him saying:

"Do not be afraid. I am the First and the Last. I am the Living One; I was dead and behold I am alive for ever and ever! And I hold the keys of death and Hades" Revelation 1:17-18.

What a victory. Death defeated. There is no time to waste. Make sure of your calling. If you are already a Christian, rededicate your life to God. If you don't know Jesus yet – then simply respond to the ever-present call God has on your life. Seek him out. *"Taste and see that the Lord is good"* Psalm 34:8.

"His Divine power has given us everything we need for life and godliness through our knowledge of him who called us by his own glory and goodness. Through these he has made us his very great and precious promises, so that through them you may participate in the Divine nature and escape the corruption in the world caused by evil desires. For this very reason make every effort to add to your faith goodness; and to goodness, knowledge; and to knowledge, self-control; and to self-control, perseverance; and to perseverance, godliness; and to godliness, brotherly kindness; and to brotherly kindness, love............ Therefore, my brothers, be all the more eager to make your calling and election sure. For if you do these things, you will never fall, and you will receive a rich welcome into the eternal Kingdom of our Lord and Saviour Jesus Christ" 2 Peter 1:3-11.

He Knows Us

Before I formed you in the womb I knew you, before you were born I set you apart;
Jeremiah 1:5

I have the path mapped out. If you could see the ports of call I have for you, they would seem as indecipherable to you as the pattern of my stars in the heavens. But I know each stop you will make along the way.

Direct word from God

Chapter Seven

Early Lessons

Back to my story.

By mid-1976, I'd met Jesus, I'd been baptised in the Holy Spirit, I was speaking in tongues and I was exercising the gift of prophecy. Although I was fully participating in my Catholic faith again, I was growing and being nurtured as a new Christian in a small vibrant Protestant charismatic prayer community. I learnt as the scripture was shared and taught during regular prayer meetings that I attended. I learnt from study and discussion sessions held during Uniting Church mission weeks. Some years later, I also learnt from attending an Alpha course run by what was by then the Uniting Church. Alpha is a ten-week course, which helps people to understand what Christianity is about. Originating within the Anglican Church in the late 1970's to support new Christians, it has grown worldwide as a powerful non-denominational evangelising tool. It introduces Jesus to both new believers or people who don't yet know God but are simply curious about Christianity. It teaches about the importance of the Bible and about prayer and faith. It was real nourishment for my faith.

Back to my early days in Wudinna, I had no idea what my future would be but I had never felt more excited about my life. London was a vague memory from a very distant past. I stopped going back to Ceduna on weekends. By the June long weekend of 1976 my journal records these momentous changes with these words:

"Christ has come."

I decided I no longer needed to fill my journal pages up with *"my introspective selfish jottings"* and dropped my writing practice. I must have thought the arrival of God in my life would solve every problem I would ever have again. That was perhaps a little over ambitious. By March of the following year, I had recommenced journalling, a practice I continue to this day.

I wasn't to know at the time but God had four years to prepare me for what has undoubtedly been my major life project – raising a family. Looking back over these years prior to my marriage, I can see that God chose to begin this preparation by challenging me in several quite specific areas of my life.

I sometimes wonder what the heavenly planning session might have looked like. I like to think of Jesus and his Father standing around a whiteboard with a few angels, brainstorming what would be most important for me to know. We've got four years to get some foundations established, they might have said. From my journals, it looks like they came up with a list like this:

~ Daily prayer and Bible reading

~ Submission to authority

~ Obedience

~ Food/fasting

~ Tithing

~ The fifth commandment

Lesson 1. Daily prayer and Bible reading /submission to authority

I had never owned a Bible. I grew up listening to scripture passages read out during Mass but I had never followed this up with any sort of personal Bible reading practice. I had no idea that reading the Bible was a direct way I could hear from God. I did not understand that the Word of God is real food.[1] The Catholic Church has a lot to answer for in not actively encouraging its members to feed on the Word of God and even worse, for long periods throughout history, actively denying their members personal access to the scriptures.

As I said previously, after my momentous encounter with God at the Saturday night prayer meeting in Kyancutta, the first Bible I read for myself was a small red New Testament published by the Gideons which I had found in the Wudinna Area School staff room. No one at that Kyancutta meeting had told me to go away and read the Bible. But in the following week, I just happened to see that little Bible sitting there on the shelf in the staffroom and I'd picked it up and taken it home with me to read. I devoured it. The words seemed to leap off the page. I thought it was extraordinary. I didn't yet know this passage of scripture but I was experiencing it in real life:

"For the Word of God is living and active. Sharper than any double-edged sword, it penetrates even to dividing soul and spirit, joints and marrow; it judges the thoughts and attitudes of the heart" Hebrews 4:12.

The first scripture that struck me deeply from my reading was about submission to authority. Even though it was the 1970s and a time of great social change, I didn't see myself as a free spirit. There was no sign of a rebellious spirit in me. I had little sense of self, and in all areas of my life I was very conservative. I wasn't journalling during this exciting period so I can't be sure which scripture it was that so captured my attention but it may well have been this one: *"Everyone must submit himself to the governing authorities, for there is no authority except that which God has established" Romans 13:1.*

At the time, despite it being a reasonable request, I had been resisting submitting my lesson plans ahead of time to the English senior teacher, as if somehow, I, a junior teacher, knew better! Closer to the truth, it was probably because I was lazy and didn't like to plan ahead. Maybe I thought I was good enough to 'wing-it'! Whatever the scripture was, it totally convicted me. I began to glimpse that the challenge of 'giving' my life to God was more complex and nuanced than the act of saying mere words. Bringing myself into a

---

1. Jesus says in Matthew 4:4 "It is written: 'Man does not live on bread alone, but on every word that comes from the mouth of God.'"

right place before God was about letting go of my own will, my own ideas about what I should or should not be doing, my own ideas about what was right and wrong.

Because of that one impactful scripture, I immediately began to comply with whatever requests were being made of me by my seniors. I truly accepted that those in authority over me, in the school environment, were representing God's authority. I accept that there may be appropriate times for civil disobedience but that wasn't one of those times.

This radical new idea that the authorities currently operating in my life were agents of God also meant I became more Catholic than ever before. Although I was growing and learning what it meant to be a Christian within the Protestant prayer community, I was still a practising Catholic and had no sense I should be anything other than that. I began to go to Mass more frequently than I had for years which was not that often given one priest served several towns across considerable distances. To compensate for this, I arranged with the priest who lived in a neighbouring town to be given permission to unlock my local church so I could take daily communion by myself outside of the Mass.

From my reading of the Bible, I began to understand that it wasn't an ordinary book. It is more than history, more than theology, more than beautiful poetry, it has magical powers. It can speak clearly to all of us in whatever situation we find ourselves. It is majestic, it is confronting, it is personal and intimately loving, a never-ending source of comfort and strength. And I regret not having spent more time across my life within its pages.

Despite everything I have learned over my years as a Christian, I often still struggle with the daily disciplines of prayer and Bible reading. So this first lesson that I believe God wanted to teach me at the beginning of my Christian walk has stayed relevant for me throughout my life. You might think that lockdowns during the early months of Covid in 2020 would have given me ample opportunity to spend time in daily prayer and sacred reading but apparently not! This message arrived in April of that year:

> *There are things you are not yet doing on a regular and consistent basis, still not committing or submitting to regular prayer and meditation, quiet reflection where you can let go of your anxieties and focus on gratitude. You know this intellectually and yet you still do not drink daily from the well, liquid gold refreshment available to you whenever you choose to*

> *avail yourself of it. Everlasting life, everlasting strength, love, beauty all available in quietness and in stillness. Go there. Sit there and then revived and refreshed go about your practical tasks. Write, clean up your debris, detritus. You think it is important but it's not as important as you think. It's reflected images of your life as it has been. I want to see you awake, refreshed, noble in your intent to face forwards. Above all, make love your standard, unconditional, blind love. Move away from critical judgments. Let go and fill your world with pure love.*

I felt resoundingly admonished, my lack of discipline in this most basic of practices, daily prayer, exposed again. And *'detritus'*! That was a shock; the word means waste or debris, rubbish! I knew what God was referring to. I didn't have a large house, or a basement, or a garage full of my life's possessions but I did have personal files and boxes of my words, including my journals and random memorabilia. I had begun to think that I should sort through all of this. It had seemed valuable to me which is why I'd hung on to all my journals for all these years, but here was God saying, no they're not!

Covid had also triggered thoughts about possible future worldwide calamities, the kinds prophesied about in the end times. I wanted to warn my grandchildren. I wanted them to know that no matter how troubled the world might seem, they could face the future with confidence by putting their trust in God. I began to think about writing the story of my journey with God as a way of helping my grandchildren.

But I was challenged by the call to love. *"Above all make love your standard, unconditional, blind love. Move away from critical judgements."* Could I do this? Could I surrender the crisp edges of my own thoughts and ideas; could I place them under the purifying influence of God's Holy Spirit? Could I write in a way that would reflect the pure love of God? I could only try.

Lesson 2. Obedience, food, fasting.

With 63% of adults and 24% of children considered overweight, it's clear that many Australians have a complex relationship with food (Aust Institute of Health and Welfare 6 March 2023).

I left boarding school overweight, due I think to a combination of boredom and poor-quality food. Hunger at day's end for boarders meant filling up after dinner with soft white bread and butter with lashings of jam or peanut butter! We would regularly hold informal competitions to see who could eat the most. I have a vague memory thirteen slices could win the day. And easy snacks after breakfast were balls of butter rolled in cornflakes! When I did leave school, I was probably about a stone and a half overweight or in today's measurements, 9-10 kgs over what was considered average for my height. I was not self-conscious about my weight at the time. I was considered tall for a girl so I wore those extra pounds well enough.

I lost that excess weight in my first year at teachers' college. My journals record I was often hungry across those student years and regularly had to wait for the next payday to do a full food shop and/or I would have to borrow money from a sister. But I was at least eating better quality food, so that combined with lack of money to buy too much of it, melted those extra pounds away!

Even though I didn't have a weight problem as such, I still had a problem with food. I used it for emotional support, eating inappropriately to comfort my lonely self, bingeing on sweet foods, consuming whole packets of biscuits in one sitting. I didn't have enough money to drink too much, so fortunately alcohol never became a problem.

Although I knew I had a few bad eating habits that would occasionally break out, I didn't think they were bad enough for God to have to intervene. Early in 1977, my second year at Wudinna, I had been berating myself after a session of overeating. God responded with this:

> *Eat less than you want to, always eat less, that is both a discipline and a sign of your love for me. I can use the morsels that you offer me. Strengthen your body in other ways through prayer and exercise. My child I am training you in many ways. Learn to submit in these outward ways you will then be better able to offer to me those parts of your inner self to which you are clinging most tenaciously. Oh, the joy that is in store for you. Would that you could see with my eyes.*

Bending my life towards Jesus, or as he put it to me, learning *"to submit in these outward ways"*, putting aside my will for his, was not proving easy. Here was God bluntly telling me that spiritual growth was not some detached esoteric thing that I could pursue whilst I kept on with a range of undisciplined behaviours. I was accountable for all the choices I was making about how I lived in my private life and God was watching.

It was the Lenten season in 1978. Lent is a six-week season when Catholics are encouraged to renew their commitment to God in preparation for celebrating Jesus' resurrection on Easter Sunday. Prayer and fasting and other acts of self-discipline are encouraged. Since becoming a Christian, I was taking these church traditions and rituals more seriously than ever. One evening, sensing God wanted to speak I heard this:

> *I am calling you to undertake a fast. Be careful that you do not make this fast your idol. It is I your God whom you are to seek. Seek me daily. I shall guide you and strengthen you, nourish you and refresh you. I would have you eat but I would have you hunger after me and so I ask for this time that remains before the celebration of my Son's resurrection, that you learn to experience a physical hunger. I promise you many spiritual blessings will flow out of this experience. Be alert to the promptings of my Spirit.*

I wasn't sure exactly what this fast was meant to look like but I decided that I would give up my lunch for Lent. I did not commit to a total fast. I couldn't quite envisage that level of abstinence! So I decided to eat one unbuttered bread roll and drink only water for my lunch. To help me avoid the temptation of seeing others eating, I left the school grounds each day at lunchtime and walked down to the Bakery and bought one of their (admittedly delicious) wholemeal bread rolls. That and water was my lunch throughout Lent. There were many days when I struggled, but the voice of God was always encouraging. For example, after one difficult day this message came:

> *Draw sustenance from our communion throughout this day.*

And further practical encouragement came when I hit another tough patch:

> *Start eating with me, not before coming to me, not after coming to me but with me. You know how people serve to moderate your eating habits, allow me to be your ever-present moderator, one who is understanding, gentle, compassionate and quietly loving. Speak to me as you eat as you would with one who was present. Punctuate your meal with our loving dialogue. Have you not been reading of my visitations to the disciples after my Resurrection? Yes, we broke bread together, we shared meals. It is a sacred time made sacred by the one true meal which I offer you each day - myself. Child, child* (spoken with tenderness).

I am writing about how God drew my attention to my relationship with food in the same breath as obedience because I think that's what God wanted me to understand. Obedience is not just an idea, a distant concept. My obedience in the area of food wasn't about weight loss. It was about drawing closer to God; it was about knowing what it meant to hunger for God. I had so much to learn about how God uses outer physical disciplines to bring about inner spiritual growth. Years later I received an explicit message to this effect:

> *Discipline- the only thing that really matters in this life is discipline for that opens the door to my blessing, my care. My love is always there for you but it doesn't always find entry into your lives. Discipline and sacrifice are like the mine sweepers, like the snow machines that clear away debris and provide access and movement to my Spirit.*

The dictionary tells us obedience means complying with an order or request. It means to submit to another's authority. Giving way to someone else can hurt. Those of us who are lucky enough to have access to unlimited food as part of our daily life, are unused to denying ourselves. Abstinence is not part of our vocabulary. Obeying God's directions to me about food was a concrete and visible challenge that I did not find easy.

The scriptures both the Old and New Testaments are full of references to fasting and the powerful role it plays in bringing us to a right attitude before God. David writes in Psalm 35:13 *"I put on sackcloth and humbled myself with fasting."*

Read about Jehoshaphat's amazing victory over the vast armies of Moab, Ammon and Mt Seir (2 Chronicles 20). Jehoshaphat, King of Judah (873-849 BC), was facing what he thought was an impossible situation. Before approaching God for help, he proclaimed a fast, not just for himself but for all the people living in Judah. Then he called the people to gather, men, women and children, and in front of the temple, he prayed to God. His entreaty ends with this beautiful verse which has become one of my favourite prayers: *"We do not know what to do, but our eyes are upon you"* 2 Chronicles 20:12. The Spirit of the Lord then fell on one of the priests and through him, God answered. It is a long and detailed answer which in summary said: *"Do not be afraid or discouraged because of this vast army. For the battle is not yours but God's"* 2 Chronicles 20:15. And that is exactly what happened, God himself set ambushes amongst the invaders and all were destroyed. It's another amazing story of how God can deliver us out of the most impossible of situations.

Read about Queen Esther (Esther 1-9). This too is a wonderful story. During the reign of King Xerxes, a Persian king who ruled between 486 and 465 BC, Haman, one of his court officials, plotted to destroy all the Jews who were living under Xerxes' rule. Once Esther, a Jew but also the wife of Xerxes, was advised of her people's dilemma, she sent a message to Mordecai (the cousin who had raised her after the death of her parents): *"Go gather together all the Jews who are in Susa and fast for me. Do not eat or drink for three days night or day. I and my maids will fast as you do. When this is done, I will go to the king even though it is against the law. And if I perish, I perish"* Esther 4:16.

Esther's strategy of seeking God's help in a difficult situation through prayer and fasting brought about a happy ending – something Jews celebrate to this day in the annual feast of Purim. Putting it simply – fasting, like obedience, is powerful in ways we can't always understand. It draws us closer to God, it clarifies our motivations and gives us a fresh ability to focus on what is truly important which is obeying the promptings of the Holy Spirit.

When I have an intractable problem in my life or when I want to intercede and pray for others who may be facing difficult situations, I will often choose to add some level of fasting to my prayers. Words are easy – denying myself food or drink or television is hard but fasting is a tested and tried strategy for seeking God's help.

However imperfect my first lessons in the importance of obedience, and prayer accompanied by fasting were, I believe those early lessons saved me from the scourge that food can be in our western world. For decades now I usually eat only when I am hungry. I consume all foods in moderation but I rarely over consume. I remain vigilant but I don't have to try hard anymore. Healthy eating habits are just that for me now – habits.

These days even health professionals have to be careful how they talk about weight issues with their patients for fear of giving offense. Despite the public sensitivity around this issue, I think it pertinent to share that Jesus chose to focus in on my relationship with food right at the beginning of my journey with him.

However, I should declare that I did have a few breakouts along the way to food freedom. Two years after the above Lenten lessons, I was struggling about something which I did not record in detail so I am not sure what I was feeling tempted about. I was living at that time with a wonderful couple who were part of my prayer community, on a farm just out of Wudinna. It was evening and for some unknown reason the water pressure in the house was very low. My hosts had set off to find out what was the cause, maybe there was a burst pipe in a paddock. I stayed, seeking God about whatever was troubling me at the time. This is what Father God said to me:

> *You in your spiritual life are like* (my hosts). *You know the pressure is down and you set off in the dark to find the source of the problem. How much easier it is with the light of my Son to guide you. Your continual disobedience in the area of food has left you open to temptation. Two years ago, my little one I spoke to you, "Eat less that you want to - always eat less" How often have you been obedient to that direction?"*

I went back to my earlier journal and there it was! I had conveniently overlooked all those early lessons in obedience and self-discipline. I may have forgotten what God had spoken to me about food but God hadn't. I was ashamed of my careless forgetfulness. Since it was to be another ten years before I notice food mentioned again in my journals, it seems I did change my ways.

I have come to understand that disobedience blocks us from full fellowship with God. If we have been prompted in some area of our life and yet ignore that and continue to seek God as if that annoying prompting was not worth responding to – then our lives will be diminished. We won't be living our best lives. God simply cannot bless disobedience.

"Does the Lord delight in burnt offerings and sacrifices as much as in obeying the voice of the Lord? To obey is better than sacrifice, and to heed (or listen to the Lord) *is better than the fat of rams"* 1 Samuel 15:22.

Ten years later, living a vastly different life, married and deep into raising a family, I found myself back again eating indiscriminately. Surprised at myself I asked: *This eating Lord? What is it all about?* I am still shocked by the directness and strength of His answer:

> *It is destructive and it is rebellious. But you are directing your rebellion and your right to make your own decisions against your own person. You see no one is going to interfere with you unless you care to listen to me. It* (I understood this to be my own private rebellion with food) *will achieve nothing, not even a strengthening that would occur if someone opposed you. You are flexing muscles but not in real combat. In fact, you have unconsciously chosen an area where you can experiment with your own power without any real fear of opposition. Petra that is cowardly! Flex your muscles in more constructive ways, even if it means facing opposition. You do not know how deep and real the fear in you is of earning other's disapproval. You do need strengthening not to be foolish or irresponsible but to be able to be fearless in a positive, godly manner. Stop this fascination that is growing in you - this preoccupation with food. It will not be good for you. Discipline yourself.*

These were strong words but I recognised the truth of the message. Angry and rebellious at the constant and often overwhelming domestic constraints operating in my life at the time, the only way I felt I could safely hit out was against my own body. And the ubiquitous cask wine had by then found its way onto my shopping list. Oh, the power parents have, to buy whatever they like, to do whatever they like. No one, not even God, could stop me from eating or drinking whatever I liked, whenever I liked! Such freedom!! But a false freedom as God made clear to me – in fact cowardly! I was deeply ashamed.

Disobedience doesn't sound like the worst sin in the world. It's not one I would think of putting at the top of my list of sins to avoid. Wouldn't murder be worse, cheating, lying, robbery, violence, drugs? Not even God mentions it in his top ten. But on closer reading, the call to obedience is wrapped around everything God asks of us. Adam and Eve's failure to obey one seemingly small request from God in the garden, to not eat the fruit of one tree when there were so many others to choose from, produced catastrophic consequences. It ended our time in the garden. It brought sin into the previously perfect created world. It brought death and decay. We lost our place in paradise.

The covenant, the agreement God offered to the Israelites once he had delivered them from Egypt was dependent on obedience. God told Moses to tell the people this:

"You yourselves have seen what I did to Egypt and how I carried you on eagles' wings and brought you to myself." God continues his message:

"Now if you obey me fully and keep my covenant, then out of all nations you will be my treasured possession" Exodus 19:4-5.

Although our own disobedience had exiled us from the original garden, God in his love and mercy was providing us a way back to himself. Through the set-apart life of the Israelites, living under a priestly system and sets of laws delivered to the people through Moses, God was setting up a model for other nations to follow. God wanted to demonstrate to all peoples who had spread out across the post-Flood world, how beneficial, how safe, how good living life could be under the guidance and protection of the one true God.

But oh dear – even though the Israelites trembled with fear from the thunder and lightning, the thick smoke and trumpets that heralded God's presence over their desert camp, fear of God was not enough to keep them from sinning. (Exodus 20:18). Even though they knew firsthand of God's amazing powers, they disobeyed regularly! Choose any story from the Old Testament or choose any nation in the world today and you will find evidence of how we humans find it difficult to obey God's laws.

The book of Jeremiah describes in terrible detail God's anger towards his people for not obeying his laws. God says to Jeremiah: *"So do not pray for this people nor offer any plea or petition for them; do not plead with me, for I will not listen to you" Jeremiah 7:16.*

And it gets worse:

"Even if Moses and Samuel were to stand before me, my heart would not go out to this people. Send them away from my presence! Let them go! And if they ask you, "Where shall we go?" Tell them, "This is what the Lord says: Those destined for death to death, those for the sword, to the sword; those for starvation, to starvation; those for captivity to captivity" Jeremiah 15:1-2.

What is it about obedience that is so hard? We're incorrigibly proud and independent, clinging fiercely to the right to make our own decisions, to make our life whatever we want it to be. We have free will – what an incredible and yet dangerous gift! Why should we listen to an invisible God figure?

If you believe in the Bible the answer is easy, we need to listen to God to learn how to live in this world because left to ourselves, we can't help but sin.

"Every inclination of his (i.e. man's) heart is evil from childhood" Genesis 8:21.

"For all have sinned and fall short of the glory of God" Romans 3:23.

In Romans 7, Paul eloquently laments the power of sin:

"I do not understand what I do. For what I want to do I do not do but what I hate I do...... As it is it is no longer I myself who do it but it is sin living in me. I know that nothing good lives in me, that is, in my sinful nature. For I have the desire to do what is good, but I cannot carry it out Romans 7:15-18. "... What a wretched man I am! Who will rescue me from this body of death? Thanks be to God – through Jesus Christ our Lord!" Romans 7:24-25.

Obedience sits at the heart of the weights and measures the Holy Spirit uses to support us as we battle to overcome the power of sin at work in our human nature, so that we can become truly *"conformed to the likeness of his Son" Romans 8:29.*

Oh, the path to living obediently under God's will is indeed littered with self-sabotage. But I wanted God to be my God. I wanted to listen. I wanted to obey. So, I persevered with following, to the best of my ability, all the food directives I received during those early formative years! Your Achilles heel might be different from mine, but God found mine, food. And it's been a fertile ground for many spiritual lessons.

Lesson 3. Tithing

The word *tithe* is a Hebrew word meaning a tenth. Tithing was law in the Old Testament and although Jesus' arrival means we are no longer beholden to that law, tithing seems to have survived as a voluntary practice for many Christians. Simply put, the idea is to give away a tenth of your income, to wherever the Holy Spirit directs. Tithing has a simple mathematical beauty about it. As a percentage-based measure, it means that depending on your means, it can be a little or a lot. A tenth does not seem a huge amount. Who could argue that is not a reasonable amount to give back to God?

I was introduced to the idea of tithing during my early years as a Christian. As a teacher, I never had a big income but tithing taught me how to give, how to be generous, how to stop thinking that everything I had, belonged to me, me, me! Tithing became a very practical way for me to demonstrate that I was indeed learning to submit important areas of my life to God. Money or food it didn't seem to matter to God. Both provided practical important lessons to me about how to move closer to God, so I could hear the promptings of the Holy Spirit more clearly.

I confess that over the years I haven't always been consistent in this practice of tithing. After my divorce, I lost faith in God and abandoned the practice altogether for many years. But despite my inconsistencies, giving remains an important practice and a discipline in my life. And I believe it has resulted in a level of comfort and financial security that I could not otherwise have expected. After all, I am a retired baby boomer who spent many years out of the workforce caring for children, then working part time and like others of my generation, I have missed out on the full benefits of superannuation.

Giving is not just the preserve of Christians. There are many generous people in my world and over the years I have been the grateful recipient of many gifts both in cash and in kind. You all know who you are and I am so grateful. I don't mean to imply that by tithing or any other spiritual discipline or practice, we can earn the grace of God. Being looked after is not something God only offers to those who 'deserve it'. Not at all. But somehow the act of regular giving opens the door to also receiving and I am grateful for the comfortable life I am privileged to now live.

"Give, and it will be given to you. A good measure, pressed down, shaken together and running over, will be poured into your lap. For with the measure you use, it will be measured to you" Luke 6:38.

Lesson 4. The fifth commandment

"Honour your father and your mother. Then you will live a long, full life in the land the Lord your God is giving you" Exodus 20:12.

The fifth commandment is the only commandment that has a promise attached to it. Throughout my story thus far, I have used the New International Version (NIV) translation of the Bible but for this verse I am using the New Living Translation because it makes the promise even clearer. Regular damaging reviews of the state of aged care in our nation confirms that this is indeed a difficult commandment to comply with. God must have foreseen this reluctance of ours to look after our ageing parents and so he's added this promise of a long, full life as an incentive.

I stumbled over this scripture sometime in the middle of my second year as a Christian, or more accurately I should say God brought this scripture to me! Just as the verse about submission to authority had impressed itself on me, so too did this verse. At the time, my elderly father was being cared for at home in Cowell by my mother. However, it was becoming increasingly difficult for her to do this on her own. The aged care industry had not yet developed sufficiently enough for it to offer any solutions that could support my mother with in-home care. Extended stays in the local hospital were becoming regular.

Meanwhile the fifth commandment was burning its way into my mind and heart. I could help. Couldn't I? I was single and 'free' to step aside from teaching and go home and help my mother. Given my status as a single woman looking for a partner, and Cowell being an even smaller town than Wudinna, this plan did not appeal to me. But I couldn't escape the conviction that this was what I was supposed to be doing. So finally I applied to the Education Department for leave of absence that would commence in the following school year. It wasn't a life sentence, I'd only applied for six months and I would see what happened after that. My application was accepted.

It was early December. My plans were all in place. End of year rituals were underway, marking completed, reports written, the school concert was about to be held. It was eight o'clock Monday morning of the final week of the school year when I got the phone call from my mother. My father had died overnight.

Even now, as I write about this I am deeply moved, not because I am sad about my father's death. It was a blessed release for him. I am moved because I had been tested and found true. I had been given an opportunity to demonstrate obedience at a level that hurt me. I had agreed to step aside from my free independent life and give my life over completely to service in the name of Jesus. I was and still am so grateful for the gift of that opportunity. It was a real test and then my mother's phone call had released me. I was overawed and grateful.

Through that experience, the fifth commandment found a deep home in my soul. Years later, this time with the support of my husband and other family members, we were able to offer a home to my husband's mother. She had dementia and was being cared for in the local hospital. We didn't visit often enough at all but on one of our visits she had begged us to 'take me home, take me home'. I suggested we at least bring her home for a weekend visit. During this weekend visit, I was helping her in the bath. Frail and vulnerable, she began to sing this hymn:

"Cover me Lord, cover me,

Extend the border of your mantle over me.

For though art my nearest kinsman, cover me" Ruth 3:9.

The song comes from the story of Ruth, the Moabite widow who chose to follow her also widowed mother-in-law Naomi back to her home in Judah. Following Naomi's advice, Ruth speaks these words to a family relative Boaz. Boaz was Naomi's nearest kinsman. According to Jewish law, this meant he had the right to marry – or 'cover' Ruth, thus securing both Ruth and Naomi's future.

It was a plaintive cry from my mother-in-law. I heard it as a direct message from God. It was true, my husband and I were amongst her nearest kinsmen. How could we in good conscience ignore her cry? And so arrangements were made to bring her home. We didn't do this alone. Another family member had been similarly convicted and she, a single mother at the time, came along with her young daughter to live with us on the farm. In our home, she became her mother's main carer for nearly three years until more specialised care became necessary.

I had one more chapter left with this fifth commandment. Many years later when my own sweet mother could no longer live safely in her home on her own, I and another of my siblings offered her our homes. I lived on a farm near Cowell where she had lived for over fifty years and my other sibling lived in a city. It was no surprise to us when our mother chose the farm. This time we did have the support of the aged care system so that I was able to remain working whilst carers came in for a few hours at the start of each weekday and then mid-afternoon, breaking my mother's solitude until I got home from the local school where I taught. My mother had a gracious spirit. She asked for nothing but the chance to help. It was a privilege but even so it was not an easy commitment. She stayed with us on the farm for nearly three years before we moved her into full time care in the local aged care centre.

That's my experience with the fifth.

In no way am I suggesting that these early lessons should be the curriculum for all new Christians. We are all unique individuals and we should listen to the guidance only the Holy Spirit can give. This sequence of learning is just how God began to work in me.

But there was one other major theme that was operating quietly in my spiritual life during these early years - where did I belong? I was a revitalised Catholic and yet I was learning about what it meant to follow Jesus and find spiritual nourishment, amongst my Protestant friends.

I think, standing around that planning whiteboard I had imagined, Jesus and the angels had neglected to spell out that they were planning to move me out of the Catholic Church!

... and by the way Petra...

WE'RE GOING TO MOVE YOU OUT OF THE CATHOLIC CHURCH

"*Sir,*" *the woman said, 'I see that you are a prophet. Our fathers worshipped on this mountain but you Jews claim that the place where we must worship is in Jerusalem."*

Jesus declared, "Believe me, woman, a time is coming when you will worship the Father neither on this mountain nor in Jerusalem. .... Yet a time is coming and has now come when the true worshippers will worship the Father in spirit and truth, for they are the kind of worshippers the Father seeks. God is spirit, and his worshippers must worship in spirit and in truth.

John 4:19-24

Chapter Eight

On Leaving

Recently, I retraced the steps of my early years as a young teacher in Ceduna and Wudinna. I called it a pilgrimage. I wanted to revisit these places where I had, as a young adult, searched for and found God. I determined to visit all the churches that had been significant to me during this time. First on the list was St Anne's in Wudinna where, after becoming a Christian, I had taken daily communion. Then came St Michael's, a remote church in the corner of a paddock in the district of Chandada that I had visited one day as I drove past. God danced with me in that church that day. It was a sacred and sublime moment. Then came Our Lady Star of the Sea, Ceduna where I had decided I could find God more easily out in the Bay rather than in the terrible emptiness of Sunday Mass. Finally I visited St Canute's, Streaky Bay, a church that hadn't been especially important to me but I thought I'd visit it anyway as I drove down the coast from Ceduna to Pt Lincoln. I couldn't get inside any of those churches on my pilgrimage. Not one of them was open, not one. That has triggered quite a lot of thinking for me about the role of churches in this modern day. They are so locked up, so empty. Old wineskins? Another way is needed. Perhaps the simple unstructured ways of the early church should be our guide. For the first few hundred years Christians met in their homes.

St Canute's was the last Church on the far west coast that I tried to visit. Streaky Bay is a beautiful town and I delighted in the short walk out to the Church which sits on a slight rise overlooking the Bay. It was a crisp but beautiful late winter's afternoon. I found the doors locked, but I dawdled outside near the Grotto which housed a statue of Mary. As I sat there quietly, not thinking of anything in particular - cue for God to speak:

> *You and I are not Catholic Petra, so you won't find me here.....* (short pause)
> *I only found you in the Catholic Church because that's where you were.*

I'm sure I grew up believing God was Catholic but I was long removed from those uninformed days. Of course, God is nonaligned. No one group can own God. Nevertheless, hearing those words jolted me. Our preoccupation with religious brands is so irrelevant to God's purposes in the world.

Back to my Wudinna days. As I have described earlier, the more I learned about Jesus, the more I read the Bible, the more observant a Catholic I became. I was seeking to obey any authority in my life at the time as an act of obedience to God. Then I fell in love with a chap who, although a Christian, was very anti-Catholic. I began to hear things about the Catholic Church I had never heard about before but not just from him. I had many lunch time meetings with an excellent teaching colleague who offered to school me in these matters. I can still see myself sitting in a classroom listening to this thoughtful chap tell me terrible things about the history of the church that I was still happily a member of. I was horrified. I had no idea of the long and shocking history of corruption and wickedness sitting at the heart of the Catholic Church. I knew absolutely nothing about the terrible history of wicked men who bought and sold their way into powerful church positions not least, the Papacy. It was so removed from anything resembling the teachings of Jesus. Nor did I know at that time that many Catholic practices and teachings have no basis in scripture.[1] Why had no one told me about this? But that was history, wasn't it?

So, having fallen in love, we proceeded to get engaged. Then the pressure came about my status as a Catholic. I prayed earnestly for direction. I will do whatever you want me to do Jesus, I said again and again. I knew by then that Catholics had no special claim on God; I believed I could follow Jesus inside or outside of the Catholic Church. Although the issue of communion bothered me. Catholics believe that when we share communion, we

---

1. Some examples: there is no scriptural support for Catholic teachings about purgatory or the assumption of Mary into heaven or the infallibility of popes or even the position of pope itself.

share the body and blood of Jesus, literally. Many other Protestant churches believe the bread and wine are shared in memory of Jesus death and sacrifice and are mere 'emblems' of Jesus. But I subscribed to the Catholic belief and so it deeply troubled me that Jesus would want me to leave this amazing gift behind. Nevertheless, I was wholly captive to Jesus and I wanted to follow him wherever He wanted me to go, even if it meant leaving my church.

I prayed – pen in hand asking for direction and the voice of truth, the spirit of truth, the one true God had this to say to me on that memorable occasion:

> *Put your hand in mine, my little one, and come with me as I show you what I am doing in your life. You remember the jetty, the barnacle encrusted supports? Do you remember how eaten away they were? You used to wonder why they still bore the weight of the daily traffic which passed over them. Those supports, my child, were never tried beyond their capacity; they were replaced - not just those that seemed in dire need of repairs, no, the whole structure needed to be rebuilt, strong new timbers. And yes, to you, it seemed to have lost its charm. Rebelliously you looked at the workmen as they carried out their appointed tasks. And yet had they not done this, you would not today be able to walk out upon the waters. You would not be able to view the dark line of the hills that at evening you have grown to so love. It is my view, my child. How many times have you recognised my splendour in it? I gave you that little jetty so that you might see more clearly my splendour, that you might experience an overflowing joy and peace as you look around at the splendour and the glory of my universe- yes even in the humble surrounds of your home. What I am saying to you now, my child is of the utmost importance. Oh, my little one, how great is my love for you now as I look upon you in your anguish. It is mine. Allow me to take it from you. Listen again little one for our walk has not yet ended. I am easing you, my child, from the structures of this church. You are clinging to its supports just as the barnacles clung to the jetty supports. My hand moves gently but there will be some pain. But I am building a finer church. I myself shall carry you to it. No forces can attack this building, founded firm as it is on my*

faithfulness. In my appointed time, I shall move all of my children. Child become abandoned.

How does one respond to such a word as that? Who is this awesome God who can reach down into our world and speak to us so clearly? Scripture answers that:

~I am the God of your father, the God of Abraham, the God of Isaac, the God of Jacob Exodus 3:6.

~I am who I am Exodus 3:14.

~I am the Lord, your Holy One, Israel's Creator, your King, Isaiah 43:15.

~God also said to Moses, "Say to the Israelites, The Lord, the God of your fathers – the God of Abraham, the God of Isaac, and the God of Jacob, has sent me to you. This is my name for ever, the name by which I am to be remembered from generation to generations Exodus 3:15.

~This is what the Lord says - Israel's King and Redeemer the Lord Almighty, I am the first and I am the last; apart from Me there is no God. Who then is like Me? Isaiah 44:6-7.

~I am the Alpha and the Omega, says the Lord God, who is and who was and is to come, the Almighty Revelation 1:8.

~I am the Lord who has made all things, who alone stretched out the heavens who spread out the earth by myself, Isaiah 44:24.

The voice of God, the great I am, the one who stretched out the heavens, brings me to my knees always.

The 'jetty' message displayed an intimate knowledge of my childhood. The township of Cowell, established in 1880, was built on the northern edge of a large shallow harbour. Matthew Flinders had sailed past it in the *Investigator in 1802*, thinking it was a lagoon, so narrow was the entrance. In 1840 it was named Franklin Harbour after Sir John Franklin who, then Governor of Tasmania, had been a midshipman on the *Investigator*. Because of its sheltered harbour, Cowell became the main port for the towns in mid to upper Eyre Peninsula. Ketches brought supplies, mail and passengers and carted out grain, wool, mail and passengers till the late 1950s, early 1960s. However the development of bulk grain handling systems including silos and road transport in the 1960's meant ketches were no longer needed and with their departure, the important role that jetties had played in regional economies was going to change.

Growing up in the 1950s-60s in Cowell, meant I caught the tail end of that time of transition. The Cowell jetty had indeed been our childhood playground. The smell of the wheat stacks mingling with the sour smell of the mangrove swamps when the tide was out, was part of my summer life.

The long causeway led out past the fish depot where the local fishermen sold their catches. It snaked its way through the shallow area of tidal mangrove swamps to where it branched into two, a smaller jetty where local fishing boats were moored and where we swam, and the longer jetty where the ketches tied up and later the prawn boats. Between these two jetties, nets were set up so the townspeople could swim safely. Two smelly, corrugated iron, roofless sheds were built along the edge of the small jetty as change rooms for the girls and boys. That was where my sisters and I had marvelled that some of the pylons were still holding up the jetty, they were so eaten away with barnacles. It was true; we had thought one day one of them was sure to break.

Then in the mid 1970s, extensive renovations to the jetties began. The old jetty we had swum off was completely removed. The economic importance of the burgeoning prawn industry demanded a bigger, better, safer main jetty. What God said to me about the way my sisters and I had angrily viewed all this construction work was absolutely true. We did not want our dear old jetty changed – not even with its barnacled encrusted supports!

Instantly I understood the metaphor. Barnacles cling to structures. They are impossible to prise off. I had no concept of what it would mean to not be 'Catholic'. It was all I had ever known. I was stuck onto the Church like a barnacle. The message made it clear to me that I would someday leave the Church. I reflected long on the final paragraph especially these phrases – *'I am easing you'*- *'I Myself shall carry you to it'*. If God was moving me out, I would know about it but it would be gentle. It did not feel right to me that I should leave under pressure from another person.

Even though I accepted that one day I would move or be moved out of the institution of the Catholic Church, I didn't believe it was to be then and as a result my engagement ended.

So where to from there? I kept up my dual 'citizenship'; I remained part of the charismatic Protestant prayer community and I remained a fully practising Catholic. In the January of 1979, I booked myself into a Catholic Charismatic Conference being held in Sydney. Here, I thought, the two halves of my soul would find peace.

I turned twenty seven a few days before I flew out to Sydney. Being single at that age was not common at the time. It had never seemed important to me before but with one failed relationship behind me, I decided that I should ask God for help. As the plane banked and turned towards the Adelaide Hills heading for Sydney, I asked God to help me find a husband. Instantly I heard this:

Petra you will probably marry a widower with children.

I was not impressed. That's no reward for virtuous living I replied indignantly. That was not my idea of a happy ever after story. But I reasoned, maybe that wasn't even the voice of God, it was unusually indefinite. I'd never heard God use the word 'probably' with me before. I dismissed the idea and for several weeks forgot all about it.

I had a wonderful time attending many sessions at this conference held on the premises of the University of NSW. Attending communal worship and prayer and teaching sessions was a great joy. I walked through the university grounds one evening greedy for a 'word' from God but I heard nothing but the quiet of a beautiful summer's evening. Later that evening I heard this:

You wanted a 'word' from me, my little one - oh how you wanted a 'word'. Learn at these times to rest easy in the largeness of my creation which is indeed my word, my most glorious word. How imperfect, yes how imperfect is your concept of a 'word'. As it passes through your mind it is blurred, it loses its sharpness, just as this instrument - the pen (the one I was using was running out) - so too your humanity my little one - a faulty instrument. But how tenderly do I love you! We walked, you and I, this evening through the grounds of this vast university, a place of learning, of wisdom. A vast maze of concrete interspersed with greenery, both expressions of my greatness. When will you learn to see this truly as I do. I am in the great. I am in the small. I am in the 'man-made.' I am in the natural. All things come from me. All things pass through me. I am all in all....... You too, my beloved, are my creation, my most dear possession. And I will lead you to your inheritance. I will lead you through 'the maze,' the circumstances of your life. You will walk at times through the concrete, the man-made, and you will see strife and conflict, but I am there. You will enter into green pastures, and you will be refreshed, you will drink deeply at the springs of living water, and I will be there.

Day after day during this conference, I was intensely aware of God's presence and filled with incredible joy. Then came the day I sat in on a session run by a Catholic priest who was speaking about the Ecumenical movement. He said it was a good development in that it helped the different denominations to focus on what they shared in common rather than their differences. However, he said, because Catholic beliefs about the communion meal differed, Catholics should not share communion in other churches. He was quite strong about this. I was shocked and troubled. I had been sharing communion regularly with my Protestant prayer community back in Kyancutta. It didn't matter to me what they thought it was. We were sharing in good faith and I figured that was fine.

Even prior to the Last Supper, from which most Christian churches have taken the communion ritual, Jesus had taught in the Synagogue at Capernaum, about how he was offering his own body and blood as real food and real drink. (John 6). To many who were listening, Jesus claiming he was the 'bread of life' was a shocking idea:

"I am the living bread that came down from heaven. If anyone eats of this bread he will live forever. This bread is my flesh, which I will give for the life of the world. Then the Jews began to argue sharply among themselves, 'How can this man give us his flesh to eat?'" John 6:51-52.

In response, Jesus doesn't soften his message but rather doubles down:

"I tell you the truth, unless you eat the flesh of the Son of Man and drink his blood you have no life in you. Whoever eats my flesh and drinks my blood has eternal life and I will raise him up at the last day. For my flesh is real food and my blood is real drink. Whoever eats my flesh and drinks my blood remains in me, and I in him" John 6:53-56.

This was such a radical message that many disciples left Jesus:

"This is a hard teaching. (They said amongst themselves) *Who can accept it?" John 6:60......
"From this time many of his disciples turned back and no longer followed him" John 6:66.*

I believed when I took communion, I was taking more than bread and wine. I was feeding on something far more sacred. But you will remember that I was by this time in my life as a new Christian, committed to submitting to the authorities in my life as if they were representatives of God, so I was deeply challenged. I was still a Catholic so this meant I had to obey the teachings of the Church didn't it?

On my return to Wudinna after the long summer holidays, I settled into the new school year and reconnected with my usual rhythm of involvement with my two 'churches'. A new minister had arrived in the local Uniting Church (all Methodist Churches were by then under the banner of the Uniting Church) and my prayer group friends invited me to join them for the welcome service. I happily agreed to that.

Catholics share communion at every service but not so in the Uniting Church. However, as I arrived at the local Uniting Church that morning, the sign was clear, it was going to be a communion service. I had not had time to reflect and pray for further guidance about the new directive I had heard in Sydney about not sharing communion. I sat there conflicted. If I obeyed the Catholic teaching in this area of shared communion, I would have to let the wafers and the tiny glasses of grape juice pass me by. How awkward. If I abstained, it seemed a high-handed judgement on my fellow Christians here in the Uniting Church. I sat in turmoil and discomfort.

As was customary, when the appropriate time in the service came, the tray of wafers was passed along the pews. I didn't know I was going to do this but as the tray went past me, I suddenly reached out and took one, letting the small round wafer sit in the palm of my hand. We all waited to be instructed to eat it together. I apologised to God, asking for forgiveness if what I was doing was in fact an act of disobedience. I promised him that before I was caught in such a situation again, I would pray for guidance and if God wanted to confirm the Sydney conference priest's message he could and I would obey. I sat there in high emotion wondering if the wafer was going to burn a hole in my hand. It didn't but when I put the wafer into my mouth, my whole mouth vibrated, my jaw, my tongue, my cheeks, my throat. It was a sensation I had never experienced before. I sat there confused and not understanding what was happening.

In for a penny, in for a pound I thought, as I waited, along with the rest of the congregation, for the tiny glasses of grape juice to be handed out. As the tray passed me, I reached out again and took one, holding it carefully in my hand until we were all instructed to drink. Again as the liquid hit my lips, my whole mouth vibrated – this sensation passing only when I had swallowed all the juice. In my confusion and high emotion, this is what I heard:

> *I am present. I am present. Do not hesitate to partake of me. Do you think my presence is dependent on the understanding of the recipient?*

I immediately saw in my mind's eye the lines of people who through the ages had lined up in multitudes of churches to receive communion. Was God more present in communion in one church rather than the other depending on the words they prayed or the beliefs they held? No. It didn't matter what people thought, the communion meal was God's gift to us and he could choose to be present in it in whatever way he wanted. Whatever we thought, whatever our theology, God was in control. And, most gloriously, I had my direction – *'do not hesitate to partake of me'*. I took this to mean I was free to share communion wherever and with whomever. Later that evening, as I prayed further and reflected and thanked God for this momentous revelation, this is what I heard:

> *I am indeed your precious Saviour; my blood shed for you; my body broken for you. How it pleased my Father's heart to show you the reality of that gift this morning. What a veil there is drawn before your eyes - yes even your eyes. You know something of my Eucharistic [2] presence, seek to know me more there in the bread and in the wine. What joys, what powers there are locked up in the Eucharist! How gladly would I shed abroad the key to all who seek me with openness, I would reveal myself. The communion table is where you must all gather. Pray that my body may become more apparent amongst*

---

2. The word eucharist derives from the Greek word *eucharistia* meaning *thanksgiving*. It is a word often used interchangeably with Holy Communion or the Lord's Supper. Some church writers say it refers to the wider service of the Mass commemorating Jesus death not just the communion meal.

believers then my life in you will become more apparent to those who do not yet know me. Share cautiously this experience of yours. Wait.

At the time of writing that was forty four years ago and although I have shared about that experience 'cautiously' a few times with others, I remained cautious. I didn't understand what God meant by wait. You can be sure I did not go to my local priest to talk to him about this matter. I mean who was I to say that God had visited me personally and said it was okay for me to disobey this particular Catholic teaching! But it seems right to share this revelation now. May it bless whoever reads this.

Even though I do not currently belong to a Christian community, I regularly include the communion meal as part of my personal prayer life. It is awe inspiring to me, to know that one day, as this scripture indicates, I will be in the presence of Jesus and this meal will no longer be needed. But until then I will continue with this sacred practice.

"For whenever you eat this bread and drink this cup, you proclaim the Lord's death until he comes" 1 Corinthians 11:26.

But is it not a communal meal you may ask? At a time when my husband and I were not within a community, I heard this and it has given me confidence that although I remain 'outside the assembly' I do not need to deprive myself of this special meal:

You do not feed on the body of my Son as much as I intend for you .... develop, cultivate the sharing of this meal together. Outside the assembly as you are, you are not deprived of this meal by my hand, only your own. It is food, real food. It is strength, real strength to both the inner man and to your physical bodies.

I didn't realise it on that day in the Uniting Church but that extraordinary revelation and experience about the presence of Christ in the wafer and grape juice, was going to free me to leave the Catholic Church. The Catholic belief about communion and about the priest being the only one who could administer this sacrament, was the only reason I thought I couldn't leave. But God had dramatically shown me that the communion meal, the body and blood of Christ, was not the preserve of any Church or any one man. He was in charge; I could leave and still share the fullness of this sacred meal outside the Catholic Church.

So the scene was set – no obstacles remained - all the right conditions were in place for me to leave. To continue this story of my leaving the church, I need to back track a little to introduce another significant thread in my story.

Marriage

On my return to South Australia after the Sydney conference, friends tracked me down to tell me the shocking news about a car accident involving a family we all knew. A young couple I had met at a Methodist mission meeting in Wudinna in the previous year had been involved in an accident, the mother and one child had been killed and another child badly injured. My Wudinna friends invited me to join them at the memorial service that was to be held in Tumby Bay. I agreed to attend the service and thought no more about it.

The church was packed and I slipped in almost late. After the sad service, I joined my Wudinna friends for the cup of tea being provided nearby by the local church community. The husband recognised me from the Bible study evenings and because on one of those Bible study nights, I had invited the family to my house for an evening meal. He spoke earnestly to me about his situation. It was at that point I remembered the words I had heard on the plane – *Petra you will probably marry a widower with children*. I was horrified. It seemed a shocking thought to have on the day of the wife's memorial service but there you have it. That's what happened. I felt unclean. I extricated myself as quickly as I could and drove back to my parents' house in Cowell for the last few days of the summer holidays. I was so distressed at my thoughts that I stopped at one of the beaches on the way home – walking my distress out of me – begging for God's forgiveness. It just did not seem right. I rang my brother when I got home. His wise advice to me was – if this is of God it will come about. If it isn't, it will disappear. So just let it go.

It's very difficult for me to reread my journals covering that exciting year of falling in love with the man who was to become my husband and whose three surviving children I was to take on as stepmother. It was a love story but a love story with an extra dimension because God's fingerprints seemed to be all over it, from his message to me on the plane about probably marrying a widower with children, to the unfolding attraction and courtship happening under the shadow of tragedy. It would involve a big commitment on my part, made more complex because there were three young children involved.

And it put on the table again, my relationship with the Catholic Church. I assumed that I would marry inside the Catholic Church. But if my local priest was going to marry me, I had to agree to bring all subsequent children up as Catholic. But given there were already children in the mix, I could not envisage having a divided household with split church attendances. So I was faced with a dilemma.

At about this time, on three separate occasions, various people shared a scripture with me from the Book of Ruth. When I received it for the third time I was sure God was trying to get my attention.

"For where you go, I will go and where you stay, I will stay.

Your people will be my people, and your God my God" Ruth 1:16.

That is the beautiful response Ruth gave to her mother-in-law, Naomi, when she was encouraging Ruth to stay in her own country, Moab, whilst Naomi a widow returned to her people in Bethlehem, Judah. To me it was saying, I was to go with my future husband, his country would be my country, his God would be my God. By this time I had already received God's word to me about the jetty, warning me that one day he was going to lead me out of the Catholic Church. It was becoming clear to me that the time had come for me to leave behind my 'country', the land of my childhood, the Catholic Church.

The local priest's letter made the decision clear for me. I didn't keep a copy of my letter to him but I guess, in it, I had laid out my intentions to marry and was asking if he would officiate. His letter made my options clear:

"Your extraordinary letter was in the safe today. Does your intended know that you are a Catholic? (sometimes I wonder, do you?)

Of course I wondered who I really was in terms of allegiance to a particular brand of religion. It seemed to me that God had gone to great lengths since I had become a Christian to help me disconnect from my Catholic heritage. I had found him amongst Protestants. My faith was growing primarily from what I was learning outside of the Catholic Church. And finally my concerns about being locked out of the full power of communion, had been powerfully, personally and uniquely demolished as I'd taken communion on that day in a Protestant church.

The letter continued:

"..in fairness to him you should tell him before things become serious, what it entails for a non-Catholic to marry a Catholic; namely that the Catholic promises to do all in her power to have all subsequent children baptised and brought up as Catholics and that she intends to practise her Catholic Faith..."

I was to tell my intended that Catholics believe their Church is the one and only Church established by Jesus. *"We respect those of other faiths but we are totally loyal to our own. .....One religion is not as good as another......."*

As I have described earlier, by this time in my journey as a new Christian, I had already gained disturbing insights into my Catholic heritage. I may have been a rather naïve and enthusiastic believer in Jesus but I already knew that following Jesus was not the same as belonging to a church. I wanted to be loyal to the call of Jesus on my life – not to a denomination. So I knew I couldn't, in good conscience, sign up to a marriage based on what the priest was telling me I needed to do. Therefore I would have to be married outside the Church, which would officially mean I was leaving my Catholic faith behind. That was a very grievous time for me. Despite what I had learnt about its past, the Catholic way of life had become even more important to me since I'd discovered Jesus: the church rituals, the beauty of the Mass, the readings, the communion meal, even the physical beauty of the churches that I sat in. It was all important to me even though none of those things had helped lead me into a personal relationship with God. The irony of that was not apparent to me at that time.

We had marriage preparation lessons in Tumby Bay with the Uniting Church pastor who had so beautifully cared for the traumatised family after the car accident. On one of the weekends down there dutifully going through the lessons, I took a break and went off for a walk along the beach. I was wrestling with my sorrow and grief at the prospect of leaving the Catholic Church. I asked God again. Is this really necessary? I mean give me a word, say something, please confirm that this radical direction is indeed where you want me to go. Or am I off track? Am I making a terrible mistake? This is what I heard Jesus say:

> *Listen to the words that (the pastor) will speak tonight. They will be as though spoken from my own heart.*

I didn't run back to the minister's home and say, 'oh I'm so excited to hear your sermon tonight, God is going to be speaking directly to me through you'. I said nothing, but I went to the Church service with a profound sense of anticipation.

Protestant churches do not usually focus on Mary but that night in Tumby Bay, the pastor did just that. He focussed on what it must have been like for the young girl, Mary, fourteen or maybe fifteen years old, to find herself pregnant and although betrothed to Joseph, not yet married. Imagine how her family would have reacted? She would have tried to tell them that an angel, the angel Gabriel, had appeared to her and told her she had found favour with God:

"Do not be afraid, Mary you have found favour with God. You will be with child and give birth to a son and you are to give him the name Jesus. He will be great and will be called the Son of the Most High" Luke 1:30-31.

Imagine a young girl saying this to her parents to explain her pregnancy? And when Mary queried how on earth this could come about since she was a virgin, the angel answered:

"The Holy Spirit will come upon you and the power of the Most High will overshadow you. So the Holy one to be born will be called the Son of God" Luke 1:35.

Mary's parents would have been appalled, horrified, ashamed. Joseph also found it difficult to accept that his betrothed was already with child. In fact he was so distressed that he decided to quietly end the betrothal arrangements until the Lord himself appeared to him in a dream and told him to take Mary home with him as his wife *"because what is conceived in her is from the Holy Spirit"* and when the baby was born *"you are to give him the name of Jesus because he will save his people from their sins" Matthew 1:19-21.*

And so I listened to the sermon that night with tears running down my face because, like Mary, I was acting in a way that many in my community, did not understand. By marrying outside the Catholic Church, I would officially be leaving it. It wasn't that my husband-to-be required this of me, this was my own decision, my own choice, my own journey, one I believed God was leading me on.

I felt outcast, and very lonely but also grateful that God was once again able to intervene and confirm for me, outside of myself, the rightness of this strange direction my life was taking. And so we married – outside the Church.

I didn't ever receive any official communication from the Catholic Church telling me I was excommunicated. I found that out years later when my elderly mother came to live with me on the farm, as I have written about earlier. She was a devout Catholic, and I decided that while she lived with me, I would take her to Mass. And so I did. At the appropriate time, we both lined up for communion. When it got to be my turn, the priest (who I had no reason to believe knew me) looked at me and said, *"You're Petra aren't you?"* I said yes. *"Well I can't give you communion, I can only bless you.'*

I allowed him to bless me but I was angry. Even though twenty years had passed since I'd made the painful decision to leave the Church, it still hurt me deeply, that Jesus, the body and blood of Jesus, given for all, was denied me on that day.

Thanks to a kind Catholic who lived on a nearby farm, my mother was able to regularly go to Mass while she stayed with me but I never stepped foot in the local Catholic Church again.

Do Not Store up Treasures on Earth

Do not store up for yourselves treasures on earth, where moth and rust destroy, and where thieves break in and steal. But store up for yourselves treasures in heaven, where moth and rust do not destroy, and where thieves do not break in and steal. For where your treasure is, there your heart will be also.

Matthew 6:19-21

But seek first his Kingdom and his righteousness, and all these things will be given to you as well. Therefore do not worry about tomorrow, for tomorrow will worry about itself. Each day has enough trouble of its own.

Matthew 6:33-34

Chapter Nine

In the Thick of it

Ending up married with seven children was not the fulfillment of some childhood dream of mine. Yet I am grateful. I feel extraordinarily blessed by this amazing gift of family. I might have missed it if God had not drawn my attention to it in such a powerful way when he said to me as I flew out over the Adelaide Hills: *'Petra you will probably marry a widower with children'*.

Playing games

Squatter

"Oh no Mum - I have to take back all these. I've given you $5,000s instead of $1,000s."

My squatter partner son assiduously picks over my money pile extracting all the notes he'd mistakenly given to me.

"Mum, can you move over that way a little bit so I can lean all over you," says another son who wants to be a spectator to the game.

Gales of laughter. I'd picked up a card that said - insect and pest attack -sell one third of all your stock. But secretly I was happy about that. It meant I would miss 2 shots. I could relax.

Another bad card arrived - local drought - puts me out of action for another round! Great! Another few moments to relax.

A scientific experiment

"I'm conducting a great scientific experiment." "What about," I ask? *"I'm making a whirlpool."* (He's stirring his tea.) Peals of laughter. *"It is - it is. This lady told us if your parents tell you off for playing with your spoon - you could tell them about whirlpools."*

And in the background the haunting song, 'Be Glorified', plays with rich soft voices. And my lovely trio of younger boys soften my spirit and bathe me in warmth and love. Youngest son tells us we could all go to the United States, through his brother's whirlpool.

Another boy walks through the door, gangly, brown with dirt in his once white shorts, complaining of a sting somewhere. His hand searches while he tries to join in the conversation about *'Honey I shrunk the kids'*, a movie we'd recently watched. Finally he pulls out a three-cornered jack and I chide him for having no undies on.

"Mum can you give me a game now?" *"Yes,"* I say, ignoring the pull towards the laundry where the fourth or is it the fifth load of their camp clothes waits to be hung out.

"Oh dearest darling Mum," he says in half mocking delight.

Why do I ever think clothes are important!

A river runs through our backyard

A river ran through our backyard. A West Coast river. Not the kind of river you see on calendars that hang behind toilet doors. It's not that grand but rather it's a straggly river that low lying, humpbacked mallee trees and stringy barked ti-trees love to cling to — nothing grand but simply beautiful.

The Driver River doesn't really deserve the name of river. It's more a stream and although salty water can usually be found in pools scattered along its short course, it only flows after heavy rains. Rising in the nearby regions of Darke Peake and Rudall, it winds its way only a few dozen kilometres before emptying into the sea at a swampy part of the coastline south of Arno Bay. On its way, it happens to run close to the southern boundary of our farm.

One day we went for a walk along it, and for the sake of the junior members of the family, we pretended to be explorers. Our eldest son dropped us off several miles away from the house and our plan was to follow the course of the river back to our farm. Eldest son was excused. He had homework to do. Son number four regularly checked his Big Mac plastic watch. He was worried we wouldn't make it home in time for Duck Tales, then his favourite TV show.

"Keep out of the mud you kids. We've got a long way to go."

What a silly request. But we did have a long way to go, and I'd estimated it would take us at least three hours. Did I have enough distractions packed into our backpacks? Why didn't I bring more mandarins?

Although we already had favourite spots along our section of the river, we were hoping to find some new ones. And we did. In between the salt flats, we found a few lovely patches. One section even had cliffs – at least two metres high! And we found a couple of tiny waterfalls, one with a drop of at least thirty centimetres!

We picked wildflowers. No wonder they're called wild. They never look as nice tamed in our vases. We sighted our first sleepy lizards for the season; they always seem to know when spring is here before the rest of us do. We saw a snake, according to two of the boys who tried to dig it out after they'd seen it disappear into a spinifex bush.

Most of all, we created fresh memories of this delightful slice of Australia which was strung out carelessly across our backyard. We walked through stands of humble mallee trees, stringy paper barks and other ti-tree varieties, spinifex and saltbush, pigface in bloom and rye grass that tickled our noses. We ran up and down sandhills gracefully clad with an infinite variety of native plants, reflecting a balance and harmony that even the best gardeners couldn't hope to imitate.

Built across southern Australia in 1946 to protect the sheep industry from the ravages of wild dogs and dingoes, we saw the remains of a section of the original dog fence. This section had been dwarfed by the seasons of topsoil that had blown into it and wouldn't now have kept a sheep out, let alone a dingo. We had a history lesson at that spot, but not a long one. The mosquitoes were biting. How do they manage to breed in those salty waters?

In the end, we decided to forego the romance of trailing the river all the way back in favour of finding the quickest route home. The younger boys were making rebellious noises. And the Big Mac clock watcher kept letting us know that we mightn't make it back in time for Duck Tales. So we relented and called our eldest up on the UHF and asked him to drive through the neighbour's back paddock and pick us up.

And so the younger children got back in time to watch Duck Tales, while we parents put the kettle on and let the taste of our lovely afternoon linger a little longer. What a privilege it was to have a river running through our backyard.

God provides

As with any family large and small, we had our good times and our not so good times. There was always work to do and everyone was expected to help. The great outdoors was our ever-present playground. We had the farm and scrubland as the river story describes. We had safe swimming beaches on the nearby coast and we had our own slice of heaven on our own farm with a salty water hole fed from underground springs. All the children learnt to swim in that waterhole and to have fun sliding along its muddy edges.

We never seemed to have enough money but we always had enough good food on our table. Our children had only one set of good clothes but our lifestyle did not demand more. We were never able to gift our children with whatever the popular toys of the day were but they had good health, access to books and a great education.

We tried hard to teach them about God and about how important it was to trust God.

"So do not throw away your confidence; it will be richly rewarded. You need to persevere so that when you have done the will of God you will receive what he has promised" Hebrews 10:35-36.

But it was hard to teach them verses like this when the four-wheeler bike we prayed for year after year never eventuated. We had a small paddock set aside for that very purpose. All we needed was one good harvest. But it never happened. Did God not hear us? Were we not doing the will of God?

The God I have come to know is not to be trifled with or manipulated. He is not a dispenser of easy treats. He deals with us according to his plans and purposes and disciplines us in ways, we as loving parents are often reluctant to apply to our own children. He isn't afraid of major interventions and course corrections. Worried about the gradual loss of our farmland I heard this:

> *I am dismantling the outer Kingdom as I build the inner. My presence, my glory will be all you will need.*

I hated living out the reality of that word. But God directed my attention to this scripture:

"Do not be overawed when a man grows rich, When the splendour of his house increases; For he will take nothing with him when he dies" Psalm 49:16-17.

"... a man who has riches without understanding, Is like the beasts that perish" Psalm 49:20.

Yes Jesus, I said but what about having riches <u>and</u> understanding? And he replied by paraphrasing himself from Matthew 19:23-26.

> *Petra, it is harder for a rich man to enter the Kingdom of God than it is for a camel to pass through the eye of a needle.* Okay Jesus but how do I get rid of this hunger for riches? *Constantly submit it to me. Renew your mind. Be transformed through the renewal of your mind.*

I was in awe that Jesus was paraphrasing scripture to me again –but this time not just his own words but the words of the apostle Paul recorded in Romans:

"Do not conform any longer to the pattern of this world but be transformed by the renewing of your mind. Then you will be able to test and approve what God's will is – his good pleasing and perfect will" Romans 12:2.

I shouldn't be surprised but it is amazing to me to think that Jesus knows the words his apostle Paul wrote even though they were written after Jesus had ascended into Heaven.

A few days later Jesus spoke to me again. I'd been talking to him again about my love of all the world has to offer.

> *Petra this world and all its pleasures are not for you. I will gift you with many experiences, many resting places but keep your eyes on me and on the heavens and all that you need will come to you without seeking. Seek for eternal riches. I'll take care of the rest.*

I can't preach a prosperity gospel; that's not my experience of life with God but graciously on many occasions, God provided for our needs in miraculous ways. Short of cash, we hadn't let one of our children sign up to go on a school trip. However, at that time, friends were passing through. Without knowing specifically about our cash flow problems, as they left, they felt prompted to empty their wallets. The amount that fell out was twenty eight dollars, exactly the amount needed for the school trip. Who else but God could have provided that for a young boy.

Our old station wagon broke down. We needed to replace that with a larger vehicle. Of course we prayed long and hard about this. A member of our prayer community gave us $10,000. That was a huge amount far outside any budget we might have had in mind.

One Christmas, with little excitement about presents beyond the usual one for each child, friends arrived on Christmas morning from Whyalla, a larger town about one and half hours drive to our north. Their station wagon was loaded with treats that we could never afford to buy, such as chips and soft drinks plus a raft of age-appropriate gifts for each child.

Although there were excellent teachers in our local country high school, due to low student numbers at the senior level, subject choices were limited. To ensure our children had wider career choices than the local school could provide for, I wanted to send them away to the city for their final high school years. But how on earth were we to provide for that? We had no savings, no family trust fund to draw from.

All our children were hard working, capable students and all won partial scholarships for their final high school years in the city. That didn't mean they all chose to take up their offers. I was clear in my own mind that I was never going to force any child to go away to boarding school if they didn't want to. Most chose to go. Our family has been an incredibly grateful recipient of the wonderful scholarship provisions available at so many private schools through, no doubt, the generosity of past students and families. But even so it was a huge faith commitment for even with scholarship support, we still had to partially fund each child, as well as provide for all those ancillary costs that go with supporting children living away from home. But every year God in one way or another enabled us to meet those payments. One year we received $10,000 from a religious community. And once it became clear that because of the crippling interest rates on our farm debt, (up to 21% in the recession of the early 1990s that 'we had to have') we would eventually lose the farm, we strategically sold off pieces of land to support school fees. One year was particularly perilous because we had two boys who would be away at school overlapping- this meant double fees. I was so anxious – were we being ridiculous? But God said:

> *Why do you worry? If you want this, I will make it possible. Step out- walk out into the waters- they will not overwhelm you. It looks bad, yes, it is bad but look with eyes of faith. This is nothing- mere straw in the wind. Be confident, be steadfast, immoveable. Go ahead and prepare for his (the next son to go) departure.*

On that occasion, out of left field, one of my siblings generously offered significant support by hosting one of the boys for his final school year.

It was wonderful to receive a beautiful affirming letter during that time from the retired principal of one of the schools our sons attended. He recognised just how much we valued the opportunities his school was providing to our sons, opportunities they could only have had via scholarships:

"The support you offer your children is outstanding and if God responded to your needs at a propitious time through me as a vessel, then I am deeply humbled. I am glad to have had the support of the Council to assist you when you had given your all."

As I reflect on God's provision for us during those hard years, I see that although he may have been disciplining the parents, stripping us back in painful ways, he looked after our children.

I love my children, all of them. They are always in my mind and heart. I watch and pray and engage with them and their families wherever I can. They bless me regularly in many and varied ways. They are an immense treasure. They are my riches. I gave everything I had as a young woman to embark on this journey with them and for them. And yet I believe I have received so much more. They are truly my 'pearl of great price'. How blessed I have been. I thank God for them every day. And I would do it all again in a heartbeat.

However, I have chosen not to write about my children in this story in any detail. As I said in my opening explanations, in the telling of my journey with God, as far as is reasonably possible, my aim is to respect the privacy of others in my life. That includes my children. But their absence from my pages in no way reflects their deep and abiding presence in my heart and soul.

Even though I have determined to leave my children out of my story as far as possible, it would be inauthentic of me if I was to say nothing about my role as a step-parent. I spent my entire parenting life trying to make sure there were no inequities based on that fact, but blended families have their own unique challenges.

I have a step grandmother. Her name is Catherine. Catherine married my grandfather, Jeremiah Kelly, a farmer in the South Australian Clare valley, after his first wife died. There were already five children from this first marriage. Catherine then gave birth to a son, but within a couple of years, my grandfather died, leaving Catherine with 6 children to look after. My grandfather had known he was dying and had prepared his will directing that the farm was to be sold and the money was to be put in a trust fund for the education of his children. That was a noble plan and one I benefited from because of my own father's commitment to educating his family as he had been. However Catherine was only to receive a small share from the sale of the farm. I'm not surprised she left, taking her birth son with her and leaving her stepchildren to be farmed out amongst relatives. My own father also spent time in the Goodwood orphanage.

Although she died in June 1949, Catherine has been one of those from the other side who have visited me. On several occasions during my middle parenting years, she would arrive in my prayer time, always encouraging me not to take things personally. I knew that she perfectly understood any struggles that I might have been having in relation to my blended family. Rise above the petty issues of the day, she seemed to always be saying to me. For example forcing my son into a jumper to go to school was really not that important!

On a more serious note, I knew Catherine and I shared the peculiar sorrows of stepmothers who know that even though they've tried their best, that their best will never be enough. Nothing can ever compensate for the loss of the birth mother. Nothing, simply nothing. I didn't know this when I began my journey with my three older children.

During a particularly tough time I believe God gave me this scripture:

"O afflicted city, lashed by storms and not comforted,

I will build you with stones of turquoise,

Your foundations with sapphires

I will make your battlements of rubies,

your gates of sparkling jewels,

And all your walls of precious stones,

All your sons will be taught by the Lord and great will be your children's peace."

Isaiah 54:11-13

God has never used the word stepchildren with me, never. He has only ever referred to my tribe as my children. And that's how I have tried to approach my parenting life. Parenting is tough and so is step parenting. It's not at all like the Fran Fine, Maxwell Sheffield version as depicted in the American sitcom, The Nanny. However I took on the job willingly and earnestly. I believed I had been prepared by God. As I describe in the chapter detailing the early lessons God taught me, I'd been strengthened in deep and powerful ways in the first few years of my life as a Christian. I believed that taking on this ready-made family was my calling, a direct calling from God.

Fortunately my husband was a man ahead of his time. He was a very hands-on parent; he'd been mother and father to his children for a year before I arrived and so there was nothing he couldn't do. He was practical, energetic and fun loving, a very good balance to my more intense disposition. I was not often left alone. And since at that time he was a farmer, his timetable could usually be adjusted if I needed help, which I often did! Added to this readily available help, I lived in a supportive rural community and had kind and helpful neighbours.

I made sure that the older children's birth mother was always acknowledged and could be spoken about. We had the privilege of having their birth mother's sister and husband and their children living nearby for many years. That loving provision was and still is a good gift to our whole family. However, looking back now, I don't think we understood well enough how trauma works.

We didn't understand that the three children who survived that tragic car accident, (one child had also died that night along with their mother) caused by a drink driver, might need help about this at various stages of their young lives. I'm sure a better understanding of the impacts of childhood trauma would also have helped me in my parenting of the older children.

We're all adults now and I'm so proud of the journey we have all been on. It wasn't perfect, how could it be. And it's not over yet, we are still on the journey. My children, all of my children are well established, productive citizens here in Australia and around the world, working hard and deep into raising their own families. I'm so proud of them all.

And it's always a surprise to me when I occasionally remember that some of my grandchildren – wonderful young people that they are - do not actually share my DNA!

Stepping Stones 2

- Home duties for the first 8 years of marriage – typical busyness and pressures of managing a large family

- Returned to the workforce taking short term and part-time teaching contracts at first and then back to fulltime for approximately twelve years in total

- Involved in a Christian home fellowship group for about 5-6 years during this period

- We lived under constant financial stress - Interest rates on our farm debt reached 21 % during the recession of the early 1990's sealing the fate of the farm

- Left teaching to work in adult workplace learning

In the Beginning

In the beginning God created the heavens and the earth.

Genesis 1:1

Since the creation of the world, God's invisible qualities, his eternal power and Divine nature have been clearly seen being understood from what has been made so that men are without excuse.

Romans 1:20

He (Christ) is the image of the invisible God, the firstborn over all creation. For by him all things were created: things in heaven and on earth, visible and invisible, whether thrones or powers or rulers or authorities; all things were created by him and for him. He is before all things, and in him all things hold together.

Colossians 1:15-17

Chapter Ten

Why Include a Chapter About Creation?

In our loud, commercial, winner-takes-all, modern world, many people find it impossible to believe in God. Faced with the seemingly contradictory evidence of a world full of pain and suffering, and an invisible, almighty God who claims he loves us, they find it just too hard to fathom. But God has set eternity in our hearts.

"He has also set eternity in the hearts of men; yet they cannot fathom what God has done from beginning to end" Ecclesiastes 3:11.

The call of God is there always, no matter how faint it may be. And God has revealed himself to us in creation. We have no excuse for our blindness.

"For since the creation of the world God's invisible qualities – his eternal power and Divine nature – have been clearly seen, being understood from what has been made so that men are without excuse" Romans 1:20.

I'm including a discussion of the creation/evolution debate here because belief in a creator God is pivotal to my faith in God, and to his Word to us as revealed in the Bible. I believe that the steady erosion of belief in God in our modern world can be attributed to the rising popularity of the theory of evolution. Evolution is a clever ploy from the father of lies, Satan. If everything arrived on earth accidentally – emerging out of nothing and evolving slowly over billions of years into the sophisticated and intricately organised world we see today – then we don't need God. There's no room for God in such a mindless accidental world. There is no meaning to our lives, no guiding force. We are pawns in a great accidental game. No creator, no Divine lover – each man is master of his destiny and beholden to no higher power. My intention in including a discussion of the creation/evolution debate here is to chip away at the monopoly power the theory of evolution holds in our contemporary world. I want my readers to be curious enough to follow up with wider reading and consider an alternative perspective.

I have my own children and grandchildren in my mind. I don't want them to be overwhelmed by all the bad news that dominates our world. I don't want them to be so burdened and despairing about the pointlessness of it all that they lose hope and spiral down into self-harm, such that they can no longer function. Given the increasing levels of anxiety, depression and mind destroying addictions across our communities, this is already happening to many people, children included. This is why I want to talk about creation and the hope it can give us. Hope is not a weak word, it is a powerful force and we need to talk about it more.

"But those who hope in the Lord will renew their strength. They will soar on wings like eagles; they will run and not grow weary, they will walk and not be faint" Isaiah 40:31.

This hope is available to all. Knowing there is a creator God, a designer who is in charge with a plan, is a great reason to stay hopeful in our troubled world. The creation story as we read in the Old Testament, explains the reasons for our fallen world. But it also points us towards the saving grace of Jesus Christ, our redeemer, our Saviour. That's why I include this discussion right at the centre of my story.

My early understanding

I visited a zoo for the first time when I was about nineteen years old. I remember only one thing about that visit, the gorilla. Or it may have been George, the orangutan, that was a resident at Adelaide zoo from the early 1950s through to the mid-1970s. I would not have known the difference between the two species. I was standing in front of its enclosure, staring at it with great interest. I knew it was generally accepted that humans had evolved from apes, and at the time, I don't remember having an issue with that. But with fierce and unexpected clarity, I declared to myself, as I stood there, that I was in no way related to that animal. I wasn't a Christian at the time so that insight was not the result of my religious upbringing. It was just there as a sharp clear piece of information. I did not come from any kind of monkey.

I now have a much more sophisticated understanding of where I fit in the universe than I did then and I still don't believe I am in any way related to monkeys or any other kind of animal for that matter.

What do I believe now?

I believe in the theory of creation as described in Genesis, the first book in the Bible. According to this version of our history, God created the entire world and everything in it, in six days, resting on the seventh. According to studies based on biblical genealogies, this happened about six thousand years ago. My ancestors, the first humans, Adam and Eve, were created by God on the sixth day of creation along with all land-dwelling creatures. Yes, this means we walked the earth with dinosaurs!

"God made the wild animals according to their kinds, the livestock according to their kinds, and all the creatures that move along the ground according to their kinds" Genesis 1:25.

"And then God said, let us make man in our image, in our likeness" Genesis 1:26.

The phrase – *according to their kinds*- is important. It means we all arrived complete and entire inside the boundary of our kind: humans as humans, dinosaurs as dinosaurs, cows as cows, apes as apes. We all arrived with complete sets of genetic data. There would be no evolving into higher forms. And think how amazing this is, every created kind arrived with the ability to reproduce and for most this required male and female versions of each kind of creature.

Evidence in the world today shows that since that early time, the original created 'kinds' have developed untold numbers of species and sub species. Just look at the family of dogs. There are currently thought to be thirty five species within the family of Canidae, ranging from foxes, domestic dogs, wolves, and even coyotes! But this has happened through the loss of genetic information, through mutations, and through natural selection which often, according to environmental conditions, favours some life forms over others.

As well as the emergence of new species, natural selection, which is not the same as evolution,[1] can also lead to the loss of some species. (Darwin's essential mistake was equating natural selection as evidence of evolution.) We know this from the fossil records, which tell us some 'kinds' of animals have become extinct, for example dinosaurs and woolly mammoths. But loss and speciation are the results of loss of genetic information.[2] No scientist has ever yet demonstrated the ability to create new genetic material. We've grown clever in manipulating what already exists, but we can't create new genetic material.

My belief in the theory of creation puts me at odds with contemporary world views. But the Bible tells me:

"Always be prepared to give an answer to everyone who asks you to give the reason for the hope that you have" 1 Peter 3:15.

For this reason I've tried to keep informed about both theories. I refer to creation and evolution as theories rather than established truth or science, because there are no recorded eyewitness accounts of the origins of our world. No one was there to see light created on day one of creation (Genesis 1:3), or the first sunset on day 4 (Genesis 1:16). I note that according to the creation version of events, light existed before the creation of the sun and moon.

Christians who subscribe to a belief in creation as opposed to evolution, believe that the first five books of the Bible (the Pentateuch) were written by Moses, under the inspiration of God, some two and a half thousand years after the week of creation. However, given the nature of the subject matter, there is no way to carry out experiments to test the validity of either theory. So to believe in either is an act of faith built on the interpretation of sets of data that cannot be unequivocally proven to be true. That's why I call them both theories.

I am not very skilled in defending God's Word as laid out in Genesis. But I have learnt much from my reading and listening to the work of Creation Ministries International (CMI). The CMI website, and a wide range of their publications share information aimed at keeping believers up to date with the implications of the latest scientific discoveries as they relate to the creation/evolution debate.

---

1. (Weiland et al., 2014) Ch 1.

2. https://creation/speciation-is-not-evolution

CMI is an apolitical and non-denominational organisation. It aims to support churches around the world to teach and preach the truth of the Bible message. Their speakers and teachers are reputable, highly qualified scientists across various fields, including geology, archaeology, astrology, biology, mathematics and physics. They use their scientific knowledge to help us understand and defend our faith as it relates to the creation/evolution debate. And this debate is important because at its core, it is really a debate about whether God exists or not.

As well as publishing books and online material, CMI provide qualified speakers for events. I've attended many of their sessions over the years hosted by a wide range of Christian groups including Baptists, Uniting Church, and Seventh Day Adventist. I've heard many presentations including: *A brief History of Time; Creation/Evolution: Why does it Matter?* and *Evidence for Noah's Flood in Australia*. During my time in Brisbane, I went on a field trip with Dr Tas Walker who showed our group evidence of the flood in rock and soil formations in the greater Brisbane region. It was so refreshing to look at the land through the lens of creation. I have touched rock formations formed in the flood. Wow!

Christians who believe in the theory of creation rather than the theory of evolution, are not afraid of science. Science can help us better understand the world around us, thereby honouring the God who holds it all together with his love and unchanging principles and power.

I don't have the scientific expertise to talk about many of the issues that divide creationists and evolutionists. For example, I am not skilled enough to present coherent arguments about time and space. There are still many cosmological mysteries to solve. These include topics such as the formation of stars and the time taken for light to arrive from distant stars, dark energy, exploding stars and the notion that our universe is still expanding.[3] Nor do I have the ability to do justice to the finer points of biology that can show how it would have been impossible for most animals to survive unless they arrived fully formed with all their features available in good working order.[4] They would have died before evolving sufficiently to live and breathe or swim.

---

3. (Weiland et al.,2014) p.215

4. (Sarfati,1999) Ch 4&5

I definitely can't explain to you how creation scientists can show that the Big Bang Model is not the best way to explain all the phenomena in the astrological world.[5] And I can't explain to you why so many evolutionary arguments rely on assumptions that cannot be verified. In the case of the Big Bang Theory, there is an assumption that a 'primordial singularity' sits right at the start of the creative process. But if indeed the world and everything in it arrived via a Big Bang moment, it would mean that something was created out of nothing. That's hard for anyone to explain unless they believe in a creator. A creator by their very nature is well able to create something out of nothing.

But what I can describe to you are some of the key areas of evidence which have persuaded me that the theory of creation provides a better explanation of the history of our world than the theory of evolution. You can check these things out for yourself but here's my list:

1. Evolution is a theory not established science

2. There are no transitional forms in the fossil record to support evolution

3. The earth is not that old

4. Evidence that challenges belief in an old earth does exist: soft tissue in dinosaur bones; rapid formation of layers of sediment; unreliable radiometric dating methods

1. Evolution is a theory not established science

Let me begin with challenging the statement that evolution is science. The theory of evolution underpins the teaching of biology and geology and other complementary earth sciences in school curricula around the world today. It is presented as fact, as science. Nature documentaries fill our screens with glorious images of this beautiful world but all commentaries refer to it as being the result of evolutionary processes. They present the idea that this beauty, this coordinated beauty with intricately constructed life forms, both animal and vegetable, is the result of billions of years of accidental evolutionary activity. This claim that the earth is old is presented as science, as established truth and, as such,

---

5. (Williams & Hartnett,2005) Ch 4

gives evolution a level of immunity in our modern world that is hard to challenge. But let's look at the definition of science:

Science is: Knowledge about the structure and behaviour of the natural and physical world, based on facts that you can prove, for example by experiments.[6]

The Miriam Webster dictionary[7] goes a bit further:

"Science is: knowledge or a system of knowledge covering general truths or the operation of general laws especially as obtained and tested through the scientific method."

What is the scientific method? The Oxford Dictionary[8] says this: It *"means making an observation, developing an idea to explain the observation, turning the idea into a theoretical proposition or hypothesis, and then testing the theory against further observations made in a way that is replicable."*

Both creationists and evolutionists observe the world and develop hypotheses about its origins. What neither group can do is test their hypotheses with further observations in a way that is replicable. As I have written earlier in this chapter, we can't go back and try to orchestrate another week of creation or another Big Bang moment followed by billions of years of gradual evolution.

In that regard, neither creation nor evolution can be referred to as established science. Whichever *theory* you think best matches the evidence you see in the world, that's the one you should adopt. Just don't call it truth or science.

This argument was very liberating to me. It put me on an equal intellectual basis as all of those who subscribe to an alternative story about the origins of the world. I'm happy with that and I hope it helps anyone reading my story to become curious enough to explore the story of the universe through the lens of a different theory, that of creation.

---

6. https://www.oxfordlearnersdictionaries.com/

7. https://www.merriam-webster.com/

8. https://www.oxfordreference.com/

2. There are no transitional forms in the fossil records

The lack of transitional forms in the fossil records was another idea that caught my attention when I first began reading creation literature. All over the world fossils have been found buried in layers of rock and soil. Creationists believe that the fossil record is the result of the flood God brought upon the world. By using biblical genealogies and other events described in the Old Testament that can be verifiably dated, creation believing Bible scholars place the flood at about 1,600 – 1,700 years after the week of creation or to put it another way, approximately 2,300 BC.[9] From dinosaurs to molluscs, whole intact skeletons have been found trapped in rock formations all over the world. However there has never been a fossil found that represents an animal on its way to becoming a more complex animal. Even evolutionists have trouble with this fact.

Stephen Jay Gould, a well-known evolutionist said this:

"The absence of fossil evidence for intermediary stages between major transitions in organic design.... Has been a persistent and nagging problem for gradualistic accounts of evolution."[10]

The lack of transitional forms in the fossil record was a problem for Charles Darwin himself:

"Why is not every geological formation and every stratum full of such intermediate links? Geology assuredly does not reveal any such finely graduated organic chain; and this is the most obvious objection which can be urged against the theory."[11]

Perhaps the most popular 'evidence' produced over many years in support of these missing transitional forms has been the discoveries of bones or fragments of bone, even teeth that have been described as proof that humans have evolved from ape like creatures. Diagrams in textbooks showing four-legged images of apes slowing turning into upright man were based on the scanty evidence of such bone fragments. Dr Emile Silvestru in Chapter 4 of

---

9. https://creation.com/the-date-of-noahs-flood

10. (Sarfati, 1999) p.48

11. Ibid., p. 47 - Direct quote from C.R. Darwin, Origin of Species 6th edition 1872 (London) p.413

Evolution's Achilles Heels[12] discusses all this in great detail. I refer you to him. Suffice it to say, it's taken decades, but many of these fossils that were found in Africa, Nepal and in the Philippines, once considered to be evidence of our early relatives, are now considered to belong to a group of extinct apes.

3. The earth is not that old

Up until the late 18th century, most people believed the earth was young. This view was based on the genealogies outlined at length in various books of the Bible. All Christians believed this unquestioningly. Even if a few generations had been missed for some reason, taking the biblical genealogies into account, the earth could not be more than about 6,000 years old. The view that the earth must be billions of years old is a relatively recent view and came from early studies in the field of geology. [13]

There were two competing assumptions or philosophies[14] that underpin interpretations of what caused the geological formations visible across the world, uniformitarianism and catastrophism. *Uniformitarianism* is the belief that all natural features in the landscape had developed at the same pace as could be observed in the landscapes of the present-day world. (that is – very slowly)

The other interpretation of the origins of geological formations was based on a theory that allowed for *catastrophic* events. In other words the pace of what we see happening around us in the landscape today does not necessarily mean it's always been forming at that pace. Catastrophic events might have increased the speed of geological processes. Creationists have one such catastrophic event in mind, the Flood as recorded in Genesis Chapters 6-9, *"on that day all the springs of the great deep burst forth, and the floodgates of the heavens were opened. And rain fell on the earth forty days and forty nights" Genesis 7:11-12.*

The *Principles of Geology*, a three volume book written, by Charles Lyell and published in the 1830's brought together many of the early beliefs in uniformitarian ideas. Lyell was an avowed nonbeliever who quite openly claimed that one of the purposes of his work was

---

12. (Weiland et al., 2014) Ch 4

13. https://creation.com/the-origin-of-old-earth-geology-and-its-ramifications-for-life-in-the-21st-century

14. (Sarfati, 1999) p.104

"To free the science [of geology] from Moses."[15] He was referring here to the established belief amongst Christians that the book of Genesis, which describes God creating the world, was Divinely revealed to Moses.

"Lyell insisted that the geological features of the earth can, and indeed must, be explained by slow gradual processes of erosion, sedimentation, earthquakes and volcanism operating at essentially the same rate and power as we observe today. He rejected any notion of regional or global catastrophism; earthquakes, volcanoes and floods ..... By the 1840s his view became the ruling paradigm in geology."[16]

This is when the idea of an old earth took hold. And it has largely held the world captive since then despite the steady emergence of evidence that throws doubt on many evolutionary explanations. And guess who read Lyell's book as he sailed out in the Beagle? Yes, Darwin.

"Old-earth geology paved the way for Darwinism. On his famous voyage around the world Darwin studied the first volume of Lyell's Principles of Geology and then applied the same naturalistic assumptions to his interpretation of the biological evidence."[17]

4. Evidence that challenges belief in an old earth

Soft tissue found in dinosaur bones

Firstly, in 2005, Dr Mary Schweitzer, a US paleontologist, found soft tissue inside the femur of a *T. rex*. This controversial find rocked the scientific world. Dinosaurs are thought to be around 65 million years old. The discovery of soft tissue that was consistent with intact red blood cells would mean the fossil could not have been that old.

---

15. https://creation.com/did-god-create-over-billions-of-years

16. https://creation.com/the-origin-of-old-earth-geology-and-its-ramifications-for-life-in-the-21st-century

17. ibid

According to Dr Carl Weiland, of CMI Australia, *"This discovery gives immensely powerful support to the proposition that dinosaur fossils are not millions of years old at all but were mostly fossilized under catastrophic conditions a few thousand years ago at most."*[18]

To read more about the significance of this discovery and the debates it is inspiring across the scientific community, check out articles on the creation.com website.

Rapid formation of layers of sediment

The second thing which challenges uniformitarianism and more specifically belief in an old earth is evidence of swiftly forming geological formations that have occurred in the modern world.

Mt St Helen's volcanic eruption in the mid 1980's in the United States state of Washington, provides startling evidence of how volcanic activity cut deep gorges and deposited over seven metres of finely layered sediment in the matter of one afternoon![19]

Creationists believe that the story of the Flood described in Genesis provides an explanation for how the geological features of the world might have been catastrophically impacted, creating the high mountain ranges and deep valleys and gorges we see today.[20]

We are well aware in our modern world of the damage local floods do to the environment. However, it is almost impossible for us to comprehend the level of damage a worldwide flood that lasted for one hundred and fifty days would have delivered across the globe. But for those who believe the Bible, we can read in the Genesis account about the utter devastation that such a world wide flood caused.

"The waters rose and covered the mountains to a depth of more than twenty feet. Every living thing that moved on the earth perished - birds, livestock, wild animals, all the creatures that swarm over the earth, and all mankind. Everything on dry land that had the breath of life in its nostrils died. Every living thing on the face of the earth was wiped out; men and

---

18. https://creation.com/schweitzers-dangerous-discovery

19. (Sarfati, 1999) p.105-6

20. Christians also believe the flood was God's punishment for widespread sin in the world – read Genesis 6

animals and the creatures that move along the ground and the birds of the air were wiped from the earth. Only Noah was left and those with him in the ark. The waters flooded the earth for one hundred and fifty days"

Genesis 7:20-24.

Unreliable radiometric dating methods

The Bible indicates that the earth is about six thousand years old. However, radiometric dating (including carbon dating) puts the world at over four and half billion years old. So what are we to make of this significant discrepancy?

I don't understand enough to write with authority about half lives and daughter/parent ratios, or the structure of atoms. But I can draw your attention to literature that is available written by appropriately qualified scientists who can properly debate these matters.[21]

What I can understand from my reading as a lay person, is that when these dating methods are applied to rocks where the real time dates of their formation are known, startling discrepancies are produced. Two such examples are Mt St Helens, 1984, Washington State USA, an event I have referred to earlier in this chapter and Mt Ngauruhoe in New Zealand which had three separate lava flows in 1949, 1954 and 1975.[22] Results of rocks that were tested from these sites using radiometric dating throw considerable doubt around the reliability of dating methods currently used to support arguments for an old earth.

Despite increasing evidence now available that supports the theory of a much younger earth, in order to keep believing in evolution, people need to keep believing in an old earth. Billions of years are needed in order to help people believe that a single cell in some boggy swamp somewhere in our galaxy could 'evolve' into the intricate and complex organisms and ecosystems we see all around us.

---

21. creation.com website

22. (Wieland et al., 2014) p. 196-7

In summary

There is a detailed biblically based timeline available to view on the creation.com website and I refer you to that.[23] I can choose to believe in this creation-based timeline of our history or I can choose to believe that the incredible design and order that can be observed in our natural world is the result of accidental evolutionary processes that have taken place over billions of years. As I've already made clear, I'm more satisfied with the creation option.

The biblical version of our history can supply many answers to all sorts of questions, historical, scientific and moral. Thanks to the work of CMI, there is now an easily accessible library of resources available to balance the power that evolutionary arguments have gained over the last two hundred years. I invite you to pursue your own research.

A good place to start is the aptly named little book, *The Answers Book*.[24] It includes answers to the top 20 most asked questions that people have about evolution and creation. For example, are you curious about the biblical flood story? Could the story of the Flood as described in Genesis 6-9 explain why all over the world fossil laden layers of sedimentary rock can be found? Could the Genesis Flood also explain why so many diverse cultures around the world have flood stories in their oral histories?

Or are you curious about how the world came to be full of different people groups with different physical characteristics? If we are all descendants of Adam and Eve, how did this diversity come about? Yes, God confusing the language of people at the time of the Tower of Babel helps explain this![25]

Or are you curious about how we can see distant stars in a universe that claims to be young? These and other important questions are addressed from a creation perspective by CMI.

Belief in creation is important for Christians. It's not an optional idea. We can't have just a little bit of creator God and a little bit of evolution because to believe in evolution is to

---

23. https://dl0.creation.com/articles/p018/c01865/Bible-timeline.pdf

24. (Ham et al., 2000)

25. ibid. p.207-223

deny the existence of the God who reveals himself to us in the Bible. The God revealed to us in the Bible said after the final day of creation:

"God saw all that he had made, and it was very good" Genesis 1:31.

There was no sickness, no death or destruction anywhere at that time. Death only entered the world after Adam and Eve disobeyed God in the garden.[26] This needs repeating. It might have been weeks, it might have been months, but sin and death only entered the world <u>after</u> the week of creation.

However, evolution requires billions of years of death and decay in order to produce a sentient human being. According to evolutionary theory, only after billions of years of evolutionary activity, did humans finally appear.

The God of the Bible did not need the billions of years of death and destruction in order for everything he created – including us human beings – to arrive here on earth.

Open your mind to the possibility of a creator God.

---

26. Romans 5:12 Therefore, just as sin came into the world through one man,

Chapter Eleven

Thirsty

The trees. There were hundreds of them. Maybe six hundred. All thirsty. But we are tired. So we swim in our glorious salt water hole, refreshing ourselves in its cool waters and then we water the trees. I help, along with two reluctant boys. They've done it before. They know how hard it will be. I go because I want to support him. I don't want to cut myself off from the realities of his life. He planted those trees and now they need a drink. They never should have been planted in February. This is their second heat wave. I try to push my judgement away.

It is late evening when we start. I don't last long as the driver. I keep stalling the ute as we drive along the rows. The huge old water tank quietly leaks away. It's covered in patches. We see in the light that is left, that many of the young trees have already died. Were they eaten the day the lambs found their way in? Or did they die of thirst? I am thirsty but not for water and I pity them. We decide to water the shallow basins even if we can't clearly see a tree growing in it. Who knows, a root may be there trying to push a new shoot out. I hold one hose while one of the boys walks along the other side with another hose. The other boy turns the tap on and off. He drives.

The hose on the other side drops off. It is a poor connection. He pushes it back on again. A little later it drops off again.

"Was that while I was reversing? You need to hold it better." This said sharply. It is nearly dark and I can tell he's anxious. He's snapped a few times now and the easy peace of our night is broken. We are all anxious, waiting for the next mishap. And it comes. The hose again. I am indignant at his tone of voice. *"They're trying."* I glare at him across the tangle of hoses between the ute and the cart.

"I'll swop sides. I'll take the long side?"

"You will not. Definitely not," or words to that effect. I glare again. *"You don't have to speak like that. I just want to help!"*

"You don't have to question my decisions." He storms back into the driver's seat.

"You'd pick a fight over anything wouldn't you," he says, mocking and angry. I say nothing but lose myself in the hugeness of the sky, the stars and the dark patch of nearby scrub. The children pick up on the tension. I hadn't wanted to subject them to that again. I'd come out to support, not to create trouble. I am frightened at finding myself back in this place.

I water the next basin we come to and stare down into its cracked emptiness. Chunks of dried earth broken like the pieces of an Easter egg, disappear as the water pours in. The breeze lifts the edges of the fall of water, like a woman's skirt and plays with it, until lacy, it hits the earth. Drink deeply oh earth, for another day is coming that will surely drink you dry.

I feel a sympathy with these trees. I am their sister. I know them. I refresh them. I hold life in my hands. Springs of living water. Oh God let me find my own that they may nourish and sustain me, for I am dry and empty.

It is a glorious night - out there. The earth still warm from the day but a tinge of coolness in the breeze. And the stars. The sky is crowded with them. I sing, determined not to drown in the sharpness of our last exchange. I sing an old hymn. Can't remember when I last would have heard it sung but I sing it and it lifts me away from the edge. Nothing else matters. We could water these trees for ever. Nothing else matters. I am safe here in the dark with a job to do. I am not at the mercy of my mind because out here I have a job to do.

I move around the endless rows, searching in the dark for a shape, a stick or even some leaves that look alive.

"The oaks seem to be doing the best," he calls from the window.

"I've seen a lot of ti-trees that seem to still be okay too," I reply.

We are talking across the space. I will float across the space. I will not be defeated by it because God is with us. He will keep holding us together until this space is finally defeated. Of this I am confident. The night gives me confidence. Anything is possible. I keep walking and another song arrives on my lips. I do not know the words. They come in a language unknown to me but I sing them out across the pock-marked landscape of this salty patch of ground that we are endeavouring to resurrect.

We dawdled to bed. All of us. It was so hot in the house. The boys spread out looking for cool places, near fans, under fans. I eventually pick my way through bodies and find my own bed. Delicious under the new fan. I give in to all the exhaustion of the day and, with no hardness in our exchanges, we go to sleep. It seemed too hot to touch each other. And I was wary from the evening.

The middle years

During the middle years of our marriage, we shared our lives closely with a small group of like-minded local Christians. We all found mainstream church life was not enough. It was a wonderful time of community and of learning about God. Our homes were open and welcoming and there were many wonderful times for all of us. But we were ill-equipped as leaders and the pressures of farming life, looking after a large family, sharing in community, were too much especially given the increasing fragility of our marriage. The community was the first to disband. It was done decently enough but it was clear our leadership had not been sufficient. Our marriage was the next casualty.

Divorce is not uncommon in Australia. Based on an analysis ABS data of marriages and divorces over the twenty year period of 2003-2022, 44% of marriages failed.[1] The pain,

---

1. https://damiengreer.com.au/family-law/statistics/marriage-divorce-statistics-australia/#:~:text=With%20these%20figures%20as%20a,in%20Australia%20end%20in%20divorce.

the uncertainties, the financial and emotional costs that are a consequence of divorce are not insignificant. The anatomy of a failed marriage is as varied as there are marriages. There's nothing special about mine, just the slow erosion of love, death by a thousand cuts. I never planned for this to happen. There were no egregious events, just two flawed human beings. As a Christian, I believed divorce was not an option. But one day after a sad encounter between the two of us, something in me gave way and within three weeks, I had moved out of the family home.

I read in my journals of a creeping anger I felt towards God that we hadn't been able to find a solution for our interminable wranglings about the consequential and the inconsequential details of our lives. I fell out of love and no longer trusted the God who was leading me or the husband who was at my side. It's a shared story so it's not all mine to tell but what I will write about is the way that God, despite my frailties, picked me up and kept working with me.

Although I have sailed close to the wind both before and after becoming a Christian, I have never thought of myself as a sinner. I have felt shame about some of my behaviours but none would have landed me in a court of law. Even when my marriage failed, even then, I didn't really think of myself as a serious sinner. But that was before I better understood what the Word of God has to say about sin. *"For the wages of sin is death"* Romans 6:23. There is no hierarchy in the world of sin. There are no such things as 'venial' or 'mortal' sins, as I had been taught as a child. Sin is sin and the punishment is death, eternal death. We are born sinners (Psalm 51:5), and so all of us need the saving grace of Jesus Christ. But I was incapable, as the apostle Paul describes so eloquently in Romans 7, I was simply incapable of doing what seemed to be the right thing which was, find a solution for my troubled marriage within God's laws.

And so I see in my journals, anger and worse, foul language directed at God, the King of the Universe, the one who had nurtured me so tenderly and so personally and so lovingly into the Kingdom. Now I was turning bitterly against this same God.

It's such a rookie mistake to make, when things don't turn out the way we expect, to turn on God. It's a rookie mistake because how can we know, how can we fully understand the forces that are at work in our lives for good and for evil. How can we ever understand our sinful natures? That's where faith is supposed to kick in. Faith can carry us through when we run out of steam. *"Now faith is being sure of what we hope for and certain of what we do not see" Hebrews 11:1.*

I wasn't exactly a poet but fifteen years into my marriage I wrote this:

> My cosmic loneliness enfolds me again,
>
> Gently wrapping its familiar arms around my cold soul.
>
> The cold day gets colder,
>
> And I shrink inside myself.
>
> Tapping my feet
>
> I teeter towards the dark edge.
>
> What good my anger against this?
>
> No wonder I have caste you aside God.
>
> I spit the word out,
>
> With disgust – God.
>
> Of what good are you to me in this lonely
>
> Way of mine.

I was in a bad way. My faith was weak. Bad language poured out of my mouth and screaming, I was pushing God away. Cold and angry, I was gliding through the chores of my daily life, a stranger to myself. Cold and unrepentant, I asked God for help. I should have been struck down, annihilated before the holy presence of God, such was my lack of reverence but of all the things God could have said to me, all I hear is this gentle invitation:

> *Petra your bad language. You could start there. A little restraint- just a little? What about it?*

What a merciful, patient God, so understanding, so forbearing. I looked back at God with narrowed eyes and agreed to try. I'm in pain, I say. Help me Jesus, this is scary. What do you want from me Lord? What can I do to win your mercy? Talk to me Jesus. Is this punishment? What terrible sins am I paying for? Jesus what am I withholding from you? Speak to me please Jesus.

> *I am always speaking to you Petra, soft words of my love and faithfulness. Keep yourself still so that beneath the busyness of your days you will always hear the soothing melody of my love. Look at the world. You have tasted my peace. Beneath the turbulence that is all I can offer you this side of eternity. Come more deeply into me. I am your peace. Find your peace in me not in the circumstances of your days.*

But I could never hold on to those assurances for very long and a couple of months later I cried out to God again: *"Jesus, what if I give up? The load is too heavy. How can I give it to you? It's too much.... Oh God of the universe speak through the darkness. Show me where I am going."*

> *Steady, steady, steady. Just as it was with your car. (I'd probably gone for a slide on a wet road) Hold it steady. My hands are on the steering wheel. I will not let you run off the road. We are attending to the joints, to the rust, to the poison, breaking apart those (joints) that are infected. Trust us, trust us. Yes, even in the pain of your loneliness, your darkness, your unknowing. Rest, rest in the knowledge that you can do nothing now but wait and trust ...... Keep your eyes fixed on us. Look up – do not stumble. Look up.*

I was tired of the endless cycles we were caught in, unsure if I could continue. What if I don't come back from the edge this time? What if I turn my back forever? What if I am just too sick of crossing this bridge? What if I burn it? I see myself crying and turning myself over to some higher authority, putting my hands out to be chained again to polite civility, to compromise, anything to restore harmony.

I couldn't understand why it was proving so hard for us to find peace and I heard this:

> *Nothing of eternal value is won cheaply.* Why not Lord I asked? *Because it would destroy your sense of values. All things would become of equal value and that cannot be. You know the story about the Pearl of Great Price?[2] It is a mystery that you must allow me to maintain. One day you will understand all these things. I long to release to you the treasures of my Kingdom and yet as any wise father knows this must be done carefully. While all I have to give you is given freely, in another sense you have to earn it, you have to wrestle with me for in your searching and wrestlings you are preparing a place within your person where my truths and my treasures can dwell safely. It is a great paradox that I should want to give to you so much and yet I say to you: Seek - and then you shall find. Knock - and then will the door be opened. Press on to know me more and more.*

Is that all Father, I asked?

> *Yes, my lovely one.*

But I did not feel lovely.

I read Psalm 19:7-8&10

"The law of the Lord is perfect, reviving the soul.

The statutes of the Lord are trustworthy, ... The ordinances of the Lord are sure and altogether righteous.

They are more precious than gold, than much pure gold;

They are sweeter than honey, than honey from the comb."

---

2. This parable can be found in Matthew 13:44-45 Jesus was trying to explain to his disciples just how valuable the Kingdom of God is – more valuable than all our earthly possessions.

But I would rage against the idea that I should be obedient to God's laws. Your laws are not sweet to me. They are crushing me, killing me. I hate your laws.

Around this period Jesus spoke to me about the gift of endurance:

> *You are beautiful to me, even amidst brokenness I see beauty and strength. Be encouraged. You think you are no further along the track but your ability to endure is far greater, far deeper and endurance is a prize. I am building that in you. Concentrate on that quality rather than the sense of failure you have at still finding yourselves facing the same issues. Read the scriptures about endurance.[3] It is a quality that can only be developed, built up in you through experiencing the same events. If it were new problems, then it would not require endurance but rather the simpler skills of problem solving, the sleuth work in which you have already proved yourself. Do not be dismayed but rejoice.*

I think the sleuth work Jesus was referring to, was how I had consistently sought help via counselling. Throughout my middle years I had access to excellent support that helped me to identify and deal with some of the root issues that were causing trouble in my life. But it was not enough to save my marriage.

I'm sure divorce is traumatic for all families and all children whether they are grown up or not. It's a very uncomfortable thing to witness. Nothing is normal ever again. Not birthdays, not Christmas, not going home. Where was home? There are no winners.

By the time I gave up on my marriage contract, our children, all seven of them had left home. Well almost, our youngest was still in his final year at boarding school. Not an ideal year but I seemed to have no control over delaying that. I had no ability to wait one more year.

I was relieved to be out of the constant wrangling, the painful loneliness of an unhappy marriage but I did not expect to lose God. That absence was wide and deep, the gap, the space was shocking. I was brought very low. I'd always been able to turn to God in times

---

3. (James1:2-4), (2 Corinthians 1:8-9)

of trouble but this time I felt God had catastrophically failed me. Whose voice had I been listening to? Hadn't he led me into this marriage? Why hadn't I been given enough of whatever I needed to cope? I couldn't understand. As I have written earlier, I did not then understand the full catastrophe of sin and how it seeks to bring us down. I lost faith in God and slipped into a very dark place.

Many people in my wider network stepped back. It must have been too hard for them to understand my behaviour which seemed so obviously outside God's laws. To be fair, I had stepped back too and had withdrawn from fellowship. I barely understood my own behaviour. However, I had friends and family who did reach out to me. They kept me wobbling along, but I found no comfort in God. He was not a refuge or a tower of strength to me. I did not turn to him except with angry recriminations. It was a difficult time. I fled my home state, taking a job offer in Queensland – as if somehow the sunny climes would be balm to my soul. They weren't, not initially at any rate, although Queensland does have a lot to recommend for itself.

I have to say this upfront. As you can see, I've heard messages from God about a lot of things across my adult life but I never ever once heard God say to me, yes now you should leave, now it's time to divorce your husband. Not once. In fact to the contrary, I knew I was disappointing Jesus, Father God and the Holy Spirit. I knew they were sad about what was happening.

> *I am sad to see how things have turned out for you (both) You see it is always sin that spoils the blessings I have prepared for you ...Petra, the Father and I are grieved at what is going on, move gently and quietly. Let everything that passes through your lips be from me. Give your hurt to me..... resist bitterness at all costs. Sweet one- how it grieves me to see you both hurting as you are. You need to continually bring your brokenness to me. There is no other answer but that found in me. I can do this thing... focus on me... remember you were created primarily for relationship with God; seek that first and you will find new shades of peace in your (marriage) relationship....*

I felt sad too, desolate and terribly careless. I seemed incapable of the change required. Scriptures are clear that marriage is for life. When Jesus was asked about this, he referred to the instructions recorded in Genesis that Moses had received directly from God.

"Haven't you read, he replied, that at the beginning the Creator made them male and female, and said, for this reason a man will leave his father and mother be united to his wife and the two will become one flesh..... Therefore what God has joined together, let man not separate" Matthew 19:4-6.

The disciples went on to ask Jesus why then, had Moses allowed divorce.

Jesus replied, "Moses permitted you to divorce your wives because your hearts were hard. But it was not this way from the beginning" Matthew 19:8.

My heart must have been too hard. The Word was not strong enough in me to save me. However I am grateful that Jesus' death on the cross covers all. His love for me remained as tender and compassionate and wide and far reaching as ever. I don't want to labour long over those distressing years, but rather I will try to keep the focus on the key themes to which I think God was trying to draw my attention.

I was hungry for love there was no doubt about that. There were many messages where God tried to open me up to his love, his extravagant love spread out across the landscape of the world, the only love that could truly nourish me.

For example one day as I was walking along a beach:

See the waves? Yes Father. *Is there ever a day when they do not break upon the shore? So it is with my love. In unceasing waves it breaks upon you.*

Father, what can I do for you?

Absorb my love.

I had lost myself. Who was I if I was no longer wife or mother? Yes, I still had children but as young adults, they no longer needed the close care of a mother, especially one whose behaviour was so confusing. I had a lot of growing up to do, individuating as I was, late in life and out of season.

So managing my hunger for love and finding a new identity as a single woman were the key issues of my post-divorce life. However, before I write in more detail about them, I will write about the things that delivered healing and helped me find my feet again: poetry, work, wider reading, music and the soft beauty of Queensland itself.

Losing My Way

Petra, Petra – heart of my heart, breath of my breath.

How I miss the easy days of our fellowship. You are bitter at the journey I have led you on. Trust me again.

Unfold, unravel, uncurl, trust me again, heart of my heart.

Always, always I have your best interests before me. You need to trust me again.

Return, return to me.

Come, come again into the house of my Father.

Girl, child, woman of my heart

Return to me.

Direct word from God

Chapter Twelve

Things That Helped Me Heal

Poetry helped

I'm not really one for high literature even though I was an English teacher and that's kind of expected of English teachers. Along with my students, I learnt about literature and the powerful devices writers can use to convey their message. During the painful time after my divorce when I found no comfort in God, I found poetry helped. I understood and appreciated the power of metaphor. Metaphor elevates understanding, it increases the decibels of any kind of message. Metaphor has a power that is above and beyond the normal parameters of everyday English. It is both powerful and subtle. Metaphor can build shortcuts into truths we've managed to hide even from ourselves. That's what happened during my most painful years, I took refuge in poetry.

I missed the physical space and beauty of the farm terribly, so I read Wordsworth, *Lines composed above Tintern Abbey*:

These beauteous forms,

Through a long absence, have not been to me

As a landscape to a blind man's eye:

But oft, in lonely rooms, and mid the din

Of towns and cities, I have owed to them

In hours of weariness, sensations sweet.......

... while with an eye made quiet by the power

Of harmony, and the deep power of joy,

We see into the life of things

As I slipped away from God, I read John Donne's poetry:

Batter my heart, three-person'd God, ...

......And bend your force to break, blow, burn and make me new............

......For I, Except you enthrall me, never shall be free

Donne's powerlessness against sin, felt like mine. I was supposed to be 'betrothed' to God's laws and therefore to my husband and yet I had drifted from both:

Dearly I love you and would be lov'd fain,

But am betroth'd unto your enemy;

Paul writes similarly in Romans 7 about the terrible power of sin and yet I couldn't face the scriptures but I could read about the depths of my powerlessness against sin in poetry.

I read Emily Dickenson. Her poetry spoke to me of my own longing – for love.

My river runs to thee:

Blue sea, wilt welcome me?

....

Say, sea,

Take me!

Or this:

Not with a Club, the Heart is broken Nor with a Stone –A Whip so small you could not see it I've known

More Dickenson- these two lines fed my hungry soul:

Who never wanted, — maddest joy Remains to him unknown.

My brother introduced me to the poetry of Rumi, a Persian poet, scholar and mystic from the 13th century:

Longing is the core of mystery

Longing itself brings the cure

The only rule is, suffer the pain

Your desire must be disciplined, and what you want to happen in time, sacrificed.

More Rumi:

Empty the glass of your desire so that you won't be disgraced.

I did not want to hear about suffering or sacrifice. I wanted peace and harmony and love. But Jesus answered me:

> Break open your heart to me constantly. I can pour out healing as you pour out your troubles. I cleanse. I heal, but you must stay broken and open.

I did not want to be broken.

And of course I read Kahlil Gibran. His poetry speaks of love, longing, pain and suffering, loss and the endless mysteries of life and death. So of course I read his poetry. But his gentle exhortations to trust love were lost on me. Why should I trust love, God's or otherwise, when I thought it had left me desolate – shattered my dreams and laid waste my garden.

Oh they were hard, hard days.

And I read Francis Thompson's *Hound of Heaven,* one of my father's favourite poems. What an image, God our Father is the relentless hound who won't give up the chase. We may reject God and blame him for our troubles (as I was) and yet God says:

All which I took from thee I did but take,

Not for thy harms,

But just that thou might'st seek it in My arms.....

And the sad irony in the final verse of Thompson's poem:

Ah fondest, blindest, weakest,

I am he whom thou seekest!

Thou dravest (drives away) love from thee, who dravest (drives away) Me

When we most need God, we have a terrible tendency to drive him away. That's what I mean about making a rookie mistake. It is at our lowest when we most need the love of this forgiving and madly contradictory God, that we often turn him away. I would rail against God, regularly dissolving into sorrow. I sensed one day God trying to reach me - inviting me to come to him more deeply:

Look at me – Look at me Petra.

"*No,*" I screamed – "*people die when they do that.*"[1] *Why would I want that?*" I was clinging to my own dreams of love- of life- wealth – happiness.

"*Haven't I lost enough? Done enough? Been obedient enough? My own goodness and beauty hidden, wasted, unrecognised, rejected. I want to be mainstream,*" I screamed out to God. "*I want you to go away and stop pestering me. You have failed me- betrayed me- now go away!*"

I was wild and disconsolate, and reading Eckhardt Tolle. Perhaps he could help me where God hadn't been able to. But no matter how hard I tried to absorb his exhortations, my pain was no illusion. It seemed real and powerful to me. No longer even trying to manage my bad language, I would swear badly in whatever small motel room I was living in.

Work helped

Work kept me outwardly busy and it gave me that all important contact with people. I was in Queensland by then - travelling to rural businesses selling training programs and staying in motels but often ending my days rocking on the floor in pain. Despite my inner pain, I was so grateful for my job. Every few weeks would see me out on a road trip, north to Bundaberg, south to Stanthorpe and west to Roma. I would visit rural businesses and shire councils that had expressed an interest in the training programs the business I worked for could offer their employees. Along the way, the landscape was a gift and a helpful antidote to my inner pain.

One of the happy surprises for me in rural Queensland were the rivers. There was always a river to be found and usually a well-constructed walking path. I was in Miles one night and unlike the Goondiwindi river walkway which had been busy with walkers, joggers, and bike riders when I had visited, this track was deserted. The only company I had were the animals. I heard white cockatoos noisy with the squawk of their evening jostling in the tall trees. I heard frogs and cicadas and I saw kangaroos hopping away from me. I was in my own slice of heaven. In a clearing against the night sky, I saw a family of kangaroos – poised, ears alert ready to leap. I squatted low in the bushes to reduce my presence and drank in their delicate beauty.

---

1. Read Exodus 19 and 20. The Israelites knew that to see God or even hear his voice would mean death. They said to Moses, "*Speak to us yourself and we will listen. But do not have God Speak to us or we will die.*" Ex 20:19

The moment stretched out over me and filled me with gratitude. Such generosity from the universe! It seemed I could thank the universe but was still avoiding acknowledging the name of God. In one day I had overtaken grain trucks, passed silent headers in crops, smelt crates empty of cattle and now I had my fill of the shy beauty of kangaroos at dusk. I was content.

When the family of kangaroos moved on, I kept on walking, reaching an historic grave site cordoned off from the scrub by a ring of rough boulders. I read the dates on what was left of the sadly vandalised tombstones – 1909, 1920, 1911 and one caught my eye, George Andrew Hervey's eulogy to his wife born 1868 died 1920.

Gentle in mind, patient in pain

My dear wife left me heaven to gain

With actions so noble generous and kind

Few in this world her equal to find

Not gone from memory not gone from love

But gone to her father's home above.

I was so moved to read about her. I stood there silently in the scrub thinking about how much I'd like someone to write words about me like that after I am gone.

It wasn't often that training companies bothered to deliver training programs to regional Australians, so my sales pitches were usually well received in most of the towns I visited. But not even my clear and orderly presentation was going to win the day in Eidsvold. My contact at the council so clearly disapproved of my divorced status. He shouldn't have even known those personal details about me except he wanted to know what a woman of my age was doing travelling alone away from domestic responsibilities. Yes exactly! They were my thoughts too.

His direct questioning of me that day was unnerving and unexpected. I wasn't sure enough of my own recent choices to defend myself. And I hadn't yet moved far enough away from my old life to not remain just a little envious of him and those of his ilk. I had lived out my married life in a rural community where men like him filled community leadership roles in their weekday jobs and then preached from pulpits on Sundays sure in the knowledge of God's favour. But it hadn't worked out for me and short of interviewing his wife to get her version of this rosy picture of the 'proper' order of things, there was no way I could confirm or deny the sure and certain judgments that poured so easily out of his mouth. Within that conservative Christian framework, he had managed to hold the fabric of his life together and I hadn't. Nothing sure held me anymore. I stayed calm and circled the conversation back to the training needs of shire employees. By the time I left his office, I was sure we wouldn't be doing any work in Eidsvold.

I missed my children. I hadn't factored that in when I accepted a job offer in Queensland. I know children are naturally meant to leave their parents but I also knew that I'd left them. I'd been so wrapped up in my own pain that I'd been unable to consider how my decision to leave my marriage might have been affecting them. I didn't know how to engage with them anymore. I felt deep shame and grief about that. The enormity of my changed circumstances regularly defeated me. There were many moments when I wouldn't have said no to death. It didn't matter where I was, walking along rural rivers, the stony beaches of Bargara or on the boardwalks of the Brisbane River, the dark edges of my loss and grief wound themselves tightly around me. And when I ran out of tears, I would find myself rocking.

Joan Didion's memoir,[2] written in the year following the death of her husband, *The Year of Magical Thinking*, tracing as it did the unstable and irrational thought patterns that can accompany grief and loss, drew words on the pages of my own loss. But she had a respectable reason for her deep sorrows; her husband, her soulmate and lover had died. My grief seemed tarnished and ignoble compared to the sparse pure landscape of which she wrote. After all, hadn't I brought this on myself?

Reading helped

Early in my time in Queensland, my brother and my sister-in-law had picked up on the darkness of my crying heart. My brother came north for a visit. As we walked and talked our way around the river precinct where I was living, he took me into St Paul's bookshop. I invited him to recommend something for me to read. I waited as he browsed the shelves.

---

2. (Didion, 2005)

I knew with absolute confidence that whatever he chose would be the right book for me. Eventually he took down off the shelf a large tome, *The One Light- Bede Griffiths' Principal Writings.*[3]

Bede Griffiths was an English Benedictine priest and monk who midlife went to India. Originally, he intended to set up a Christian monastic community with a fellow monk. Although that was not successful, he stayed in India for the rest of his life becoming an internationally renowned spiritual teacher, writer and holy man. I'd never heard of him but my brother thought his writings might help me. I dutifully began reading. I could only manage a few pages each night, it was so dense. I'd never read anything like it before. I liberally used stick-it notes to try and wrestle understanding from what I was reading. I'm sure I only grasped less than one percent of his teachings but it was enough for me to push the door ajar for God to return.

I still can't say exactly which part of Bede Griffiths' compilation broke through to me. I can only say it revolutionised the way I thought about God. It broke open the character of God for me. It presented me with a bigger, larger, less easy to understand God. Paradoxically, at the same time, he reduced the scaffolding that has built up around the message of the Gospels to a simpler message – that Jesus Christ is Lord. This, he proclaimed, is the foundation of our faith. So much of the rest of the edifice is just that – structures built by human hands.

Whilst challenged, I was not convinced by all of Griffiths' perspectives. He was not in favour of the 'exclusivism' of many mainstream religions, naming three key offenders: Christianity, Judaism and Islam. He envisaged a new church – a more ecumenical church where the focus would be on experiencing Christ. Spirituality would be expressed within different cultural settings, but all would be guided by the same Spirit of Truth that Jesus promised us. This church of the future would bring together the gifts of all streams of spirituality including those from eastern religions. That was a radical thought to me.

But ecumenism sounds like a good thing doesn't it? Well it was for me, back in the 1970's when it opened me up to attending a Protestant prayer meeting where I first encountered the living God. Shouldn't we be respectful of other cultures, other traditions, other religions? Inclusion, diversity, respect, these concepts are promoted as the way forward in

---

3. (Griffiths & Barnhart, 2001)

our modern world. But Christianity is the only form of spirituality east or west that claims a leader who is the Son of God and who has defeated death.[4] This puts Christianity in a league of its own.

The apostle Paul was undoubtedly the most powerful early Christian teacher and preacher. Perhaps we should take our lead from him. He spent three years preaching the gospel message in Ephesus. During the time of Paul's ministry, Ephesus was a beautiful city, the fourth largest[5] in the Roman Empire It was a sophisticated centre for commerce, travel and the worship of the goddess Artemis.

However, Paul did not try to align himself with those who worshipped pagan gods. He did not try to make room in his developing theology for multiple forms of worship. On the contrary, his preaching of the one true God caused such trouble that he was eventually tried and expelled from the city. Too many new Christians were burning their pagan scrolls and no longer buying the silver idols the city craftsman made (Acts 19).

Similarly when he visited Athens, Paul was *"greatly distressed to see the city was full of idols" Acts 17:16.* He set about preaching about the one true God, not only to his fellow Jews in the synagogue, but also in the marketplace to whoever happened to be there. There were many highly educated people living in Athens at that time who liked nothing better than to talk about philosophy and religious matters. But they found it hard to understand what Paul was saying (as indeed do so many non-believers today). What is this babbler trying to say, they asked. He seems to be advocating foreign gods.

Some of them invited Paul to join them in the Areopagos[6] to talk further about his new ideas. How did he respond? In the memorable story told in Acts 17, we read about how Paul, having noticed an inscription to an unknown God amongst the many idols around the city, chose that as his teaching entry point. He told them he knew this unknown God. However, he did not offer this God as an extra, just another God to add to the already extensive Greek pantheon of Gods. Paul presented with simplicity and certainty, a succinct summary of the gospel message.

---

4. (Kumar & Sarfati, 2012) p. 154

5. https://livingpassages.com/riot-ephesus/

6. This is where the custodians of matters relating to gods and religious ideas met

"The God who made the world and everything in it is the Lord of heaven and earth and does not live in temples built by hands. And he is not served by human hands, as if he needed anything, because he himself gives all men life and breath and everything else. From one man he made every nation of men, that they should inhabit the whole earth; and he determined the times set for them and the exact places where they should live. God did this so that men would seek him and perhaps reach out for him and find him, though he is not far from each one of us. For in him we live and move and have our being" Acts 17:24-28.

This God, he went on to tell them, was not like one of the gold or silver or stone images that they were used to worshipping. That time was over. They would need to repent of the errors of their ways or face a coming time of judgement. Some may find Paul's approach harsh and even disrespectful. After all he made no attempt to accept or respect the local culture or local beliefs. He acknowledged their beliefs but only so he could show them a better way. Was he inundated with people wanting to follow this lone God? No – only a few were persuaded but as we know from history, that did not deter Paul.

I am writing in detail about Paul's approach because the call to be inclusive and respectful of everything about diverse cultural and people groups is promoted as a virtue in our modern world. We are called to celebrate diverse cultural practices regularly in our communities. We no longer talk about idolatrous practices. In fact to raise a voice against any such contemporary pagan practices is to invite condemnation from the world.

The Roman Emperor Constantine was the first 'ecumenical' leader. He called all branches of the early Christian church together at the Council of Nicaea in 325 AD. There, Constantine, although not yet baptised even though for overt political pragmatic reasons he had converted to Christianity, declared Christianity would now be the official religion of the empire. The problem was Jesus taught that his followers although sent 'into the world' were not to be 'of the world'. (John 17) Constantine was an ambivalent Christian at best and pagan at worst. He himself continued to worship the popular Roman pagan sun god, Sol Invictus. The fruits of this early ecumenical movement, this alliance between the church and the state, has produced much tension and confusion for Christians across centuries. To whom should their allegiance go? To the state or to God? Or was God's authority expressed through the laws of the State. This tension remains with Christians today.

I am wary about moves towards unity for all religious and spiritual traditions. How can I believe there are many different ways to God when Jesus said, *'I am the way'? John 16:6.* Scripture is very clear that the only path to God is through Jesus. As Jesus walked through towns and villages teaching about salvation and eternal life, someone asked him about this:

"Lord are only a few people going to be saved?" Jesus replied: *"Make every effort to enter through the narrow door, because many, I tell you, will try to enter and will not be able to" Luke 13:23-24.*

This is quite shocking. But Jesus went even further to make his point very clear. He said people will be knocking at the door (of heaven) pleading to be let in but the owner of the house (God) will say:

"I don't know you or where you come from. Away from me, all you evildoers!" Luke 13:27.

It's all about a relationship with God through Jesus. No amount of good living will get us through that door. Ecumenism could well be the trojan horse that lets in beliefs and practices that are not grounded in the message Jesus preached. As on the ark, when at the time of the Flood God first saved a remnant of humankind from total extinction, there was only one door; so too it is for us, Jesus is our one door.

Bede Griffiths lived much of his adult life advocating for greater understanding and tolerance between all spiritual traditions. Towards the end of his life, he was asked to describe the way he prayed. He said very simply, "*Lord Jesus Christ, Son of God, have mercy on me, a sinner.*" [7] To my mind, ecumenism needs to start and end with that declaration.

However, back then during these searching years, I was not settled on Jesus. I went on to read from other spiritual traditions. I especially liked the practical advice about how to live at peace with the world and myself that western Buddhist teachers presented. Even the titles of their books seemed to convey sensible pragmatic advice. For example the titles of Pema Chodron's little treasure of a book, *Start Where You Are,* [8] and Jack Kornfield's,

---

7. (Griffiths & Barnhart, 2001) p. 271

8. (Pema Chodron, 1994)

After the Ecstasy, The Laundry, [9] were wise lessons in themselves. It's all well and good, they seemed to be saying, to lose oneself searching for eternal truths, but we also need to learn to function in the world and be reconciled to whatever our situations might be. But none of their writings brought me back to God.

Although the door for God's return was ajar, I was still suspicious of this God I had been following. Like the Israelites who had so angered God with their high places, their altars to foreign gods, I too kept on searching in all sorts of places for ways to reduce the emotional pain then dominating my days. I explored the Runes. The Runes is an ancient form of seeking wisdom and insight about situations or questions we might have. I heard the words – constraint, necessity and pain. That's not what I wanted to hear. I had Beethoven's 9th symphony playing in the background at the time, his glorious music spilling over me. I willed it into my being, hoping that its uplifting final message about the brotherhood of man might take away my pain. It didn't.

I tried EFT. Emotional Freedom Techniques is a type of therapy that uses tapping on the body's acupressure points to relieve blockages that might be impacting your life. It aims to release negative emotions, fears and anxieties. It did not help me.

I went to a Black Moon workshop. I took notes as I listened to the presenter but I struggled to make sense of what I was hearing. It was as though I was listening to a totally different language. I heard about historic archetypes of both the female and the male. But it did not resonate with me and I did not go back.

The friendly and encouraging beautician I used to visit on Racecourse Road when I first landed in Brisbane was kind to me. She helped me to stop biting my nails down to the quick and along the way, introduced me to the books of Wayne Dyer. They helped. As Bede Griffiths writings opened the door for me to return to God, so did Wayne Dyer's stories about how God intervened in his life and work. And my dear friends, the motel managers in Hamilton, Brisbane, where I lived on and off between road trips for nearly 6 months, offered me friendship and wine.

Later, during my time in Sydney, I began to read Richard Rohr. He is an American Franciscan priest writing from within the Catholic Church and his writings have taught

---

9. (Kornfield, 2001)

me much. I fell back into my first love with Jesus because of one of his books in particular, *The Universal Christ*.[10] Richard Rohr holds a special place in my faith journey.

Music helped

Classical music has formed the soundtrack of my life. Growing up I heard my father singing the great tenor arias around my childhood home. My most requested night-time piece of music was Tchaikovsky's Capriccio Italien which my mother would play on the family piano. When I was too young to have much to cry about this piece of music made me cry.

Radio, and later the arrival of a record player in my childhood home built on that early foundation. My move to Brisbane meant that for the first time in my life I could explore live classical music. I was quick to build that into my life. I slowly built up a small circle of friends but I mostly went to concerts alone.

Sometimes, despite the beauty of the music, it was hard to listen to for other reasons. One night, I was sitting between two couples. Out of the corner of my eye, I saw one of the men take hold of his partner's hand. They did that a lot throughout the evening, her hand on his knee, his fingers knitting themselves silently into hers. That, combined with the glories of Beethoven's Symphony No. 3 Eroica, made the evening unexpectedly hard to handle.

Another time, I was at a concert featuring the music of Haydn and Schubert. I didn't know Haydn's Piano Concerto in D but the pianist, Geoffrey Lancaster, made that piece dance and play all over my soul, unlocking all the tears I hadn't cried for days. I sensed God brought Haydn down into the concert hall there in Southbank that night to witness the effect his music could have on new ears like mine.

How does music have such power, I wondered, that it can go straight to our innermost being and touch our very souls. The last piece that evening was Schubert's Symphony No 5, music I knew well. I was quite undone. Fortunately no one was sitting on either side of me so I could cry without being noticed. As the glorious music fell over the hall, all my

---

10. (Rohr, 2019)

sorrows and losses rose to the surface, my home, my place, my children, I missed them all terribly.

Then I heard God's voice insistent and strong:

You must forgive me Petra.

It was true; I had been holding God responsible for all my sorrows. I believed I had been Divinely led into my marriage. And yet as the all knowing, all powerful God he claims to be, surely he would have known my marriage was going to end badly. He would have known that my best would not be enough. So of course I had held God responsible. However, the notion of needing to forgive God was strange to me. Then the same words came again - strong and urgent.

You must forgive me Petra. Say it out loud each day. You know how the spoken word can bring things forth.

So would I? That was the question I took away from that concert. Would I respond? The next evening I tried. I began: *"Father, Son and Holy Spirit, I forgive you for...."* But that was as far as I got before a torrent of accusations poured out of my mouth, dreadful bitter accusations that I can't repeat here. Two nights later I tried again:

"I forgive you God of the universe for.... the way things turned out."

But again, that was as far as I got. Angry recriminations kept pouring out. It was another full week before I was able to humbly speak out a prayer of forgiveness to my God.

Nowhere in scripture have I read instructions about humankind needing to forgive God for anything. On the contrary, he deserves our thanks and praise for the mercy he shows towards us. If I'd lived under the law at the time of Moses and had approached God's presence in the tent without a clean heart and clean hands, I'd have been slain on the spot!

But it seemed to be working. I could feel my heart softening and so I kept up speaking out words of forgiveness to the Divine for some weeks. Looking back, I think God was helping me to surrender to him everything in my life, my disappointments, my hopes and dreams for the future. Surrender is a big word and perhaps God knew that with so much anger still in my heart, I would have tossed that word back. Somehow the invitation to forgive was easier! How extraordinarily gracious and merciful is our God.

"The Lord is compassionate and gracious,

Slow to anger, abounding in love.

He will not always accuse,

Nor will he harbour his anger forever;

He does not treat us as our sins deserve..."

Psalm 103:8-10.

The issue of forgiveness remains a regular visitor to my prayer life. Offering genuine and lasting forgiveness to those who offend us can be a challenge. Recognising my own sinful reactions in these situations, keeps me humble. Indeed, I understand better now that it's my own sin that hold me captive more than the sins of others against me. Yes, forgiveness is a complicated business.

Even the disciples struggled with the idea of forgiving others.

"Then Peter came to Jesus and asked, 'Lord how many times shall I forgive my brother when he sins against me? Up to seven times?' Jesus answered, 'I tell you, not seven times but seventy-seven times'" Matthew 18:21-22.

There is no end to the number of times we may need to forgive others. If some matter rises up, prickling our soul, then we need to bring that again and again before the Divine grace of God asking for insight about what is blocking the love and compassion of Jesus from flowing through us, so that we can truly forgive that person, those people, that event. We might need to do this repeatedly, as often as needed without keeping track of the number of times we do it.

The words in the prayer that Jesus gave us, the Our Father , remind us of this:

"and forgive us our sins as we forgive those who sin against us.' Luke 11:4 *(New Living Translation)*

There's a connection there. If we want to be forgiven for our sins then we have to pass that forgiveness on to others. The testimonies of others who have suffered deeply and yet have been able to practise forgiveness are powerfully instructive.

Queensland's beauty helped

I was reading Jack Kornfield's book about forgiveness. I'm not sure which one it was. Maybe it was *The Art of Forgiveness, Lovingkindness and Peace*.[11] I didn't make a note of the title but in a way all his books are about forgiveness. Of course I was melancholic! And I hear Jesus cut in:

> *Everybody hurts. Remember that song?*[12] *What have you really lost? A lot of sad memories. Your life on the farm was full of consolations, but they were consolations. Remember your deep inner pain and unhappiness, your disciplined efforts to 'hang on'? You have been delivered from those unhappy times. Yes, they were punctuated with consolations, trees, water, coastlines, but the joy they gave you was magnified because of your deep inner unhappiness. They were not in themselves intrinsically unique or precious. The landscape is always there for you to enter into. Do that. Take yourself there in Queensland. You have resolutely steeled yourself not to enter this landscape for fear of your grief. But I have brought you here, amongst other things, to relish the beauty and diversity of my earth. You can indeed learn to be nurtured and nourished by this. Bring to a halt this morbid attachment to the mallee! Yes, yes it has a beauty of its own but there are many other similarly deserving trees on this earth - despite what the doomsayers proclaim! I give it to you. I wait for you patiently to meet me there. Delight in this possibility, reach out, step out, meet me in my splendour - my Queensland splendour! Enough, enough of sorrow. Follow what your*

---

11. (Kornfield, 2008)

12. (R.E.M., 1992)

mind is telling you. You are healthy and that is the best gift of all. That gift leaves you free to enter all that life offers. Take it, seize it, cherish it. Enough of sorrow and mourning. That season is over. Arise now and face a new day.

So many times my journal records my answer to a word such as this – Wow! And THANKYOU in capital letters. I remain in awe. God was essentially saying – enough whingeing Petra! Get on with the good life I have given you.

I can't say I've always obeyed that clear instruction to put aside sorrow and step forward into my future alone and confident but it was a significant breakthrough. I was still living in Brisbane but I had started to live a new life and was even beginning to enjoy it. I was making friends, work colleagues and others. I joined a small group of women writers who wanted to meet after the weekend workshop where we'd met. Two of them are now published writers and I'm full of admiration and respect for them – go girls! Supported by this loose coalition, I began to write a fictional love story that would have a happy ending. That's one of those rejected manuscripts sitting in my top drawer. It was a good time for me.

I began to appreciate the beauty of the Queensland environment. I was no longer travelling out into the regions. I'd taken a city-based job managing a Registered Training Organisation (RTO). I was in awe of Moreton Bay fig trees. I walked amongst them often in the Botanic Gardens. In misty rain they seemed to have the power to speak to me in ponderous tones, like the giant trees of Lord of the Rings. They spoke of sacred things, of the inevitability of sorrows and the importance of endurance. They seemed solid and reliable and their drooping adventitious roots spoke to me about hope and opportunity. I took dancing lessons from a couple of work colleagues and I joined a dating company. This was before the digital age arrived. My heart wasn't really in that and one poor experience was enough for me to drop that venture. I had a niece living nearby whose kindness and friendship was a special gift to me during this vulnerable time. She introduced me to the restorative beauty of North Stradbroke Island which I could get to on a weekend under two hours via train and ferry.

It came time for me to move on. I was an effective, capable, workplace educator, facilitator, networker. I could design systems and implement them. I got on well with most people. I was creative and yet practical. I got the job done. However by then it was clear to me that if I wanted to catch up on my personal finances and superannuation, I couldn't sit around in the same workplace for too long. Relying on yearly consumer price index (CPI) pay increases would not be enough. I made up my mind to apply for new jobs that would substantially increase my pay every 3-4 years. But I did not leave my career progression to chance. As an educator, I practised what I preached and I regularly updated my skills with relevant post graduate qualifications. I also believed that ongoing learning would likely keep me relevant in the workplace as I aged. I'd completed a Masters in Professional Education in my final years on the farm. In Sydney, I completed a Post Graduate Certificate in Business, surprising myself by learning how to read company balance sheets, income and cashflow statements. Maths had never been my strong suite so I was extremely impressed with myself! The soft beauty of southern Queensland had done its job; my life was stabilising. It was time to move closer to family. I had children and siblings in both Adelaide and Sydney and so I started applying for jobs in both of those cities. My first job offer came from Sydney so that's where I headed.

Coming Home

*C*ome away with me – break free

New ways of thinking

The most crushing paradigm that men and women are locked into

The notion of love

There is a world far bigger than you have ever entertained

And my offer to you is to walk with me

It is not an either or but fuller, richer, wider, deeper.

You need to let go of your idea of love – the one that invades your dreams and your waking hours

Rise above

Look at the far horizon and see my enveloping love played out extravagantly across the earth and the fabric of the lives of my children

My beloved children, rise above

Direct word from God

Chapter Thirteen

The Search for Love and Identity

Michelangelo's David

It was 8.00am in Florence, Italy. The early morning queue was in good spirits. I was there in the line with a group of girlfriends. We were sightseeing in central Italy before I was to go on to visit one of my families in Europe. The morning was still fresh although with two unbroken weeks of high summer temperatures, that wasn't expected to last for long. The line of tourists could have been mistaken for beach goers. Everyone was casually dressed, in thongs, singlets and the like, except we were in Florence lining up outside the famous Galleria dell 'Accademia, home to some of Italy's most famous works of art.

Small groups along the line chatted amongst themselves. Introductions were made. Stories exchanged. Conversations and laughter rippled up and down the line. The occasional teenager looked sulky. The doors were expected to open at 8.15am. When that didn't happen some broke away from the line to find coffee. The parents of the teenagers went looking for the nearest public toilets.

"We'll hold your spot," we said.

Once the doors opened, the intimacy of the queue disintegrated and the various parties made their way into the cool spaces of the Gallery. We snaked our way around the corridors looking for David. That was the big draw card for us, Michaelangelo's famous statue of David.

Turning a corner into the long hall, I involuntarily gasped. Even at a distance, David commanded the room. With my friends, I moved forward. It was still early in the day so there wasn't much of a crowd. We had an excellent opportunity to stand and gaze.

To my surprise I began crying, sobs rising from somewhere I had no conscious knowledge of. Embarrassed, I signalled to my friend who was standing next to me, that I would move back to regain control of myself. But I didn't, I dissolved further. I can cry with the best of them but I was not prepared for this sudden uncontrollable sobbing.

My friends and I had been happily eating and drinking our way around Florence for several days. There was simply nothing going on in my current life that was worthy of tears. I was at a loss to understand what was happening. An American man, camera around his neck, stepped over to me and whispered to me:

"I've been watching you," he said. *"I saw your reaction when you turned the corner. Don't worry – this happens to a lot of people".*

I had no idea what he was talking about and must have shown it. He nodded towards David – *"he can have this effect on people."* He patted me on the shoulder and moved away.

We stayed a long time in the David space, drinking in the beauty that Michelangelo had captured in that creamy stone. I regained my composure. All I could think of as a way of explaining my tears was that I'd lost the men in my life. I'd been divorced for several years by then and despite efforts to engage, I'd had no partners along the way. I have sons – a lot of sons, glorious in their young manhoods but they had left home and were spread out across the country and indeed the world, establishing their lives and families.

Standing there in front of David in the full glory of his maleness, my loss seemed wide and terribly deep. David represented everything good about men that I missed: their strength, their courage, their beauty and their ability to act and do. I'd never touched my loss as keenly as I did there in the Galleria on that hot Italian summer's day.

On love

"There is a god shaped vacuum in the heart of every man." It is thought that Blaise Pascal, a French mathematician philosopher and all-round genius, said this after he converted to Christianity. This space can only be filled by God, he said. However I've always thought a regular earthly chap would be quite acceptable!

My search for a partner was a steady preoccupation for me in my early post-divorce years. A man wouldn't have to do much to win me. He only had to pay me passing attention or do some kind deed and he could win my heart. Offering me a cup of tea could qualify. I could build stories in my head around the smallest act of kindness.

During my shy days at university, I was smitten with one of the leaders of the Catholic student society. But as I have described earlier, I was not one to take the initiative and five years of boarding at an all-girls school had left me painfully shy around chaps. He'd probably only said hello! He never knew about my silent adoration, although he did feature in my fantasies for many years.

Another hidden crush lasted for nearly one whole university year. I would make sure to study in the same spot on the second floor of the Barr Smith Library because that's where I always saw a particular young man. Week after week we would be sitting in the same area. I sometimes went into the library on weekends expressly in the hope that I might see him. We never so much as exchanged a word. I was very skilled at silent adoration.

The thing about following Jesus is he knows everything. He knows our thoughts. He knows what's going on in our hearts. It might have been fine for me to build love stories in my mind as a single woman but God didn't let me get away with anything so dangerous in my marriage.

> *Don't dally in your mind. Learn not to loiter. It is as dangerous as walking unprotected in dark parts of a city. You simply would not make yourself as vulnerable. If you value your life then do not put yourself at risk in your mind...... do not let yourself grow casual. Be alert at all times. Guard yourself. Magnificently shelter under my wings. It is a battle of real substance...... Your obedience is required always. Rid yourself of these fantasies.*

> *My truth unfolds and it never matches your fantasies. Discern between prophetic dreams and fantasies.*

'*Rid yourself of these fantasies*' – be obedient! I was being called out by God for what was in my mind and in my heart even though I may not have been acting out my daydreams. I was and still am so grateful for God's gracious protection during times when I wanted to throw off 'the yoke'[1] of God's laws. Over my struggling years, I needed further course corrections through similar warnings:

> *You hear the birds Petra you see the birds daily feasting in the trees. That is how I would have it with you. Feast on ME. I alone can satisfy the hungers that are surfacing in you. Your heart is not convinced but by faith believe it, proclaim it, lift your vision higher.*

and more ....

> *Dalliance - but let it be with me. Let these next few days be filled with love and joy as we meet each other -renew our relationship. I am looking forward to it. Come with joyful expectation to my table. I have much to share with you.*

I demanded answers from God. "*Tell me Lord what is the secret of love,*" I asked. His answer shocked me:

> *Death.*

---

1. (Matthew 11:28-30)

If love meant death for Jesus, why should it be easy for me? *"For whoever wants to save their life will lose it, but whoever loses their life for me and for the gospel will save it"* Mark 8:35.

Sydney

I assumed that post-divorce I would partner up again. Of course I would. I would be good at love - next time around. I could be chosen again. I could find love again. And when it didn't work out for me in Brisbane, I assumed I would find love in Sydney.

I did put more effort into my search during my time in Sydney. In fact a friend and I thought we'd write a book about it. Although both of us were divorced, we liked men and missed their company. We called our proposed project, *In the Company of Men*. We even developed and circulated a survey to try to find out what men and women around our age bracket 50's-60's were looking for.

In 2008, Bernard Salt had published his amusing book, *Man Drought*.[2] I'd read that with interest – given the concept of a man drought was my lived experience. He used census data to highlight regions in Australia where the highest numbers of singles could be found. He was focusing on the age bracket between 25-34, the time in life when the majority of us partner up. His research showed that the highest numbers of young single men were to be found in mining towns whereas the highest number of single females in that age category were to be found in trendy inner-city suburbs of Melbourne and Sydney.

I thought I'd do a Bernard and so I examined the most recent census data. I searched for single men and women within the age bracket of 50-70 who were living alone. I thought living alone would be a good indicator of availability. My analysis quickly revealed that single women living alone in NSW post codes surrounding Sydney where I lived at the time outnumbered men 2 to 1. That was very disheartening. No wonder my friend and I were both having trouble finding suitable male companions. Unless I moved to the Northern Territory or the Cocos Islands, the odds were literally against me.

During this period of my life, whilst searching for the other, I read some of the classic women's literature that I'd somehow missed out on in my early adult years. I read Betty

---

2. (Salt, 2008)

Friedan, both the books of her youth, *The Feminine Mystique*[3] and the books of her older self, The *Fountain of Age*.[4] When Friedan approached her sixties she recognised her own reluctance to acknowledge that she was indeed ageing. The culture around her defined ageing as the decline towards death. Was there another story to tell about ageing? *The Fountain of Age* documents her findings, where she argues, persuasively I think, against the accepted wisdom that age equals deterioration.

I read Christianne Northrup's books on how to stay physically healthy. I also read her rollicking celebration of the life of older women, *Goddesses never age*,[5] in which she writes we need a "new paradigm" to guide us about how to live our older years. In fact, I read more books about how to age gracefully during this time than I read about how to grow in Christ.

Even though God was trying to correct my concept of love, with messages like this: *There is a world far bigger than you have ever entertained………… You need to let go of your idea of love,* I continued to reject these messages. I kept clinging to the old paradigm – the fairy story version that told me love was about 'falling in love' with one other special person and it would be magical. It would complete me, and I would live happily ever after.

I wanted God but I wanted the world too. I always had good jobs which meant I had a reasonably good income. I was able to enjoy life with financial freedom in one of Australia's most beautiful cities. This happy existence provided the ideal conditions for settling into a comfortable, lukewarm kind of Christianity, the kind that Bonhoeffer had been so concerned about. I had returned to God, but I had not returned to my first love. This time around, I had boundaries about how far God was allowed to intrude into my life. I would do this next stage of my life, my way, not his! However, God's message to the Church in Laodicea is shocking in its blunt exposure of the dangers Christians face if they become blinded by soft lives of comfort and wealth.

---

3. (Friedan, 1963)

4. (Friedan, 2000)

5. (Northrup, 2016)

"So because you are lukewarm- neither hot nor cold – I am going to spit you out of my mouth. You say, 'I am rich; I have acquired wealth and do not need a thing.' But you do not realise that you are wretched, pitiful, poor blind and naked" Revelation 3:16-17.

I am so grateful that God did not give up on me but patiently kept on reminding me about his sufficiency, and always calling me back to himself:

I have given you many loves. You are surrounded increasingly with a rich array, rich expressions of my love, my love coming to you in diverse ways. Learn to be nurtured and sustained by these loves. Enjoy it, respond, grow and blossom. All these loves are legitimate and can satisfy your soul if you will but receive, acknowledge, recognise and give thanks for......... Don't hanker for the one gift I am withholding at the moment.

And this:

Jesus, Jesus my soul is thirsty for your living waters – will you speak to me Jesus please?

I am as fresh as the morning. You cannot touch this freshness; it hangs invisible but glorious. You like to sit in the freshness of the morning - sit with me whenever you need. Wrap yourself in me. The fresh stillness of the morning. Or the warm wrap of a cloak. Children, children, how I love you. Your hunger for intimacy is but a pale reflection of my own for you. Unclutter yourself more and more and dwell in me. I can lighten your load and enliven your life, The sure and steady knowing that you are in abiding relationship with me.

The messages couldn't have been clearer. God acknowledged my hunger for intimacy, but at the same time communicated clearly that he was withholding the gift of a partner from me. I needed to be satisfied with the privilege of having an *"abiding relationship"* with none other than God himself.

I've said it before. I am an Israelite. I hear from God and yet I go my own way. In this instance, I thought I knew better. And so I did pursue relationship with a few men during my time in Sydney. One I still consider a friend and one I fell for in that truly, madly, deeply way! He'd settled elegantly into the seat beside me one late Friday afternoon on a flight heading from Canberra back to Sydney. Maybe my sharp, black Bianca Spender suit helped, for it took less than the short 40-minute flight for us to agree to meet up after our flight. I relayed every detail of this exciting meeting to my friends who duly cautioned me. It won't last, they'd said, and in the end they were right.

I knew it was probably ending as I took myself to the beach and dived into the waves. Well, there aren't exactly waves inside Sydney Harbour beaches but the slow easy lines of swell rolling in gave me a place to lose myself. I was crying as I entered the water. Like the fisherman and the mermaid, this chap and I belonged to very different worlds. As I stood later on the beach, my towel hugged around me, a strong undertow sucking the sand away from the soles of my feet, I was visited.

I didn't want to acknowledge their presence, these women, this circle of wise women who have occasionally met with me over the course of my life, usually to lift me up from a sad place. I knew they wouldn't be visiting me for a casual swim, for a light social event. No. They weren't coming for wine and pizza. Metaphorically speaking, my hands were over my ears and my eyes were shut tight. I didn't want to hear their message. This time the lead woman was my own mother. She had never been the leader among them before but on this evening, she just stood there looking kindly at me. There was a blurred circle of women around her but I didn't want to see them either.

This isn't what you need Petra.

This was delivered with a terrible kindness and all-knowing equanimity. I hated that.

This isn't what you need.

Who said anything about need! These women should have been wailing with me and using their heavenly powers to cast spells around this man that would draw him back, that would have him rushing back to me imploring me to never again move out of his sight. He should be rearranging his universe to bring this about, but no, this circle of women from heaven stood silently on the beach and allowed my mother to deliver the news - it was over.

William Blake's poem *Eternity* helped me process what had happened. I had felt chosen. Perhaps it's unorthodox to think this way, but I think Jesus allowed me to have that moment and the euphoria of a brief dalliance. And so I have kept that experience in my mind as a good gift, indeed as a taste of 'eternity's sunrise'.

He who binds to himself a joy

Does the winged life destroy

He who kisses the joy as it flies

Lives in eternity's sunrise.

It's taken many years for me to accept that God may have a different life plan for me as I live out my third age. I'm mostly reconciled with that. Occasionally I look out of the corner of my eye towards Jesus and say, "*I know, I know you're wonderful but……*" and we smile knowingly at each other.

Recently I watched one of my all-time favourite romantic movies, *Pride and Prejudice* – the Colin Firth version of course. Afterwards, as I prepared to enter a prayer time, I said this out loud to God: *"Oh I'm such a romantic!"* And quick as a flash I heard this:

> *Well why wouldn't you be! It's a love story that underpins the world, that brought your world into existence. I have filled it with love, love, love. It's there to be found - a weak pulse it may seem but my love is alive and well and continues to sustain the universe.*

On Identity

Managing my single life in healthy ways, making new friends in both of the two new cities I lived in, Brisbane and Sydney, establishing exercise routines, reconnecting with family members, all of these things were important steps in my journey back to God. Oh yes and making sure I was a productive member of whatever workplace I was in!

Although I was slow to accept God's many messages to me about finding love in new ways: *'My love coming to you in diverse ways. Learn to be nurtured and sustained by these loves.'* I did more readily grasp the messages I received about identity. Identity, so we are told, is that set of qualities and characteristics, physical and behavioural, that make us uniquely who we are. Shaped largely by our family in our early lives, it can flex and bend as we progress through our lives. It can be impacted by the events of our lives, and by social changes around us. Our answer to the question, Who am I? can change.

When I became a Christian in my mid-twenties, I took on with great excitement my new identity in Christ. I was made in the image of God! Wow!

"So God created man in his own image, in the image of God he created him; male and female he created them" Genesis 1:27.

I was chosen and special. *"But you are a chosen people, a royal priesthood a, a holy nation, God's special possession" 1 Peter: 2:9.*

And I hadn't just accidentally arrived on earth. I'd been planned in the mind of God long before I arrived. *"Before I formed you in the womb I knew you, before you were born I set you apart" Jeremiah 1:5.*

"In love, he predestined us to be adopted as his sons, through Jesus Christ, in accordance with this pleasure and will..." Ephesians 1:5.

Amazing! It pleased God to adopt me into his family! But sometimes in the fog of daily life, it's hard to remember who we really are.

I was still in Queensland and it was nearly Anzac day. I read this quote inspired by the ANZACs, *"Courage is hanging on in the face of disaster."* I asked God, *"Father God stripped of all my usual securities and comforts, will I be able to find it (courage) in you?"* Who could I speak to who would understand my devastation. I was shockingly alone in a way I had never experienced before. I cried out to God again and said, *"I never learnt to stand alone. That's it, I have never learnt to stand alone."* I had not thought about myself like this before. And I heard this:

And yes, it's hard and that's why most people never learn this rite of passage. It is considered something to be avoided at all costs and I'm giving you the opportunity to walk this way to see the sights denied so many through fear, cultural taboos, traditions. It is a fearsome journey but ah, the sights! Now I know you are not one for sights, (Jesus knew I wasn't interested in travel) *I understand that, but the internal architecture of a fully individuated human being is a wonder to behold. The Taj Mahal pales by comparison. Allow the soul to do his work (yes – her) the pronoun, as you glimpsed last week* (can't remember what Jesus was referring to here) *is not essential at all, a mere device that lacks the subtleties needed. So individuation is being able to stand alone, at peace with oneself and the world, free of need or fear or loves or grief for what was. Do not rush away but know that each storm that assaults you will strengthen and shape your inner being. Trust me, though your every instinct is to pull back.*

This was a powerfully comforting word. It helped me to make sense of the pain. I knew a little about what individuation meant theoretically, from my time in counselling. I knew it was important to grow up. Even in a partnership, it is important for both parties to have a voice, to not give too much of themselves away. Although my partnered journey was over, and I was now on my own, I knew I still had to learn to 'grow up' into my adult self in ways I had not been able to in my adolescent years. But the pain – I just hadn't expected so much pain. I understand now why many people choose not to leave unsatisfactory partnerships.

When I received this next pivotal message below about my identity, I was in the middle of a significant disagreement with some of my sons. Any hint of their disapproval would completely undo me. I knew that was not a healthy response on my part. I needed to let them express their opinions, be whoever they needed to be, without flinching so badly. I had to find meaning and purpose in my own single life apart from them! But how? Who I was apart from my children, means nothing to me, I said to God- that's the truth. And God said this to me:

You've used them as a surrogate family.

"What," I found myself exclaiming!

> *Ideally, identity is formed amongst siblings and parents in the prime unit. You never had that - floating as you did at the tail end of a family that did not, could not give you that gift of self. You've therefore unwittingly used your own family to build that identity, that sense of self and now that is being removed - the scaffolding of your adult life being removed, you are naked indeed and shivering in your nakedness. This is necessary so that finally identity can be built in truth as it should be - from within. This perilous time is necessary, trust, wait, honour yourself as best you can. Continue to do that which brings you any sort of life and comfort - diligent as always and taking the 'one step in front of the other' approach to life that you are so skilled at. Be kind to yourself and to others. Don't be tempted to place the blame for your pain on others. It is simply pain of a universal kind. Ascribe it to me if must be. Open your hands, your heart, be still and patient as we build in the darkness a new strength, a new beauty that is not dependent on your children.*

Again I was in awe of the understanding God was offering me. I knew, post-divorce, that I was "shivering" in a nakedness I didn't properly understand. I had only ever really known myself as a wife and a mother. One of those identities was gone and one was changing. Grown up children no longer need their mothers, well, not in the same way they once did. I wanted an identity that would be strong enough to hold me up in this new life. I wanted to surrender to that process. I wanted to grow. But it sounded to me as though I would have to endure the pain of this new journey patiently, taking 'one step at a time'. It was not an attractive solution at all.

I was trying to settle myself after a day's work with endless work phone calls. I wanted to be silent. I was doodling in my journal thinking of the word 'to be' Be, come, become (probably from reading Eckhardt Tolle) and then God cut in:

> *You have for so long now been focused on becoming. I want you to be. Experience being. It is such a still and joy-filled place- being. The irony is as*

you learn to be – you will become who I have envisaged for you. My ways, as always, strike you as paradoxical or full of irony. That is because I work in multiples of dimensions that are hard for you to comprehend. Being is the state where all of those multiple dimensions intersect. It is humankind's window into the Divine. Learn to be - enter the Divine. Again, (this is) another of my paradoxes. Stop searching and be.

I knew I was lucky, more than lucky, blessed to be able to hear these messages. Like ladders from heaven, they came down to me in my times of need. The mystery of God working in *"multiples of dimensions"*! I had no idea what that meant but I wanted to find out.

Leaving Sydney

Sydney is a most beautiful city but like a careless lover, it flaunts its beauty, throwing out an invitation – come and get me if you can. Sydney is hard work.

When I first arrived, I lived and worked in the inner-city suburb of Surrey Hills. Coming from leafy Brisbane, the crooked one way streets and old buildings of inner Sydney were daunting. Walking to work through random, narrow, hilly streets, I thought I'd landed in Dickensian England. It was so ugly! However, I was determined to master this unwieldy world I had jumped into.

I read John Birmingham's book, *Leviathan- the unauthorised biography of Sydney.*[6] It was a fascinating read and helped me understand Sydney's rather tortured near and distant political past and its incoherent geography. With a new friend, I walked segments of the Great North Walk, a glorious bushwalk stretching from urban Sydney north to Newcastle. Over many months, my friend and I pounded out hours of walking through a totally new landscape. And to further assist in settling in, I made myself practise my inner city driving on Sundays, when traffic was lower. I would drive back and forth across the Harbour Bridge on repeat until I caught the right exit. I had a GPS but with eight lanes and far too many exit signs, I found I couldn't rely on that to get me into the right lanes.

---

6. (Birmingham, 2011)

Although my first impressions had been unfavourable, I grew to appreciate the amazing physical beauty of Sydney and the extravagant opportunities it offered me for glorious music and arts entertainment. Sydney also provided me with the company of a much-loved sister. She and her kind and generous husband provided me with a home for my first few years in Sydney. And for the first time in my life, I had the immense privilege of joining the Day-Care pick-up roster for one of my grandchildren. Such joy! Sydney was a good gift to me in so many ways.

But despite its beauty and vibrancy and although I had built friendships with many good people inside and outside of my workplaces, and despite my loving attachment to my Sydney based family, I knew Sydney would not be my forever home. I couldn't afford to stay if I wasn't working. Since I was approaching retirement age, I knew I would soon have to return to South Australia.

Although I'd changed jobs three times since I arrived in Sydney, I'd enjoyed being settled for nearly a decade in the one city, so I wasn't looking forward to the process of being uprooted once again. In the end it was lingering poor health that pushed me to move. I couldn't shake off the colds and respiratory infections that plagued me for nearly a year. I'd even taken up winter swimming in rock pools in an effort to build up my health. But my days were simply too long. I needed to return to a city where travelling to work wouldn't be so demanding. Adelaide would give me that.

More importantly, I was finally in a place where I was once again more able to trust God with my life. Barriers were down, my heart was given again to God as completely as ever. Born again – again! I've tried to identify how this final shift back to God happened? But who can trace the work of God in the human heart? Who can see with a sure eye the infinite ways in which the Beloved seeks us out and draws us closer to himself. Who can know for sure the ways of God?

Elijah a powerful prophet who came four hundred years after the time of Moses, was very disheartened that his warnings were not being heeded by the Israelites. They were persisting in their wicked ways, worshiping false gods. In bitterly complaining to God, Elijah was indirectly asking God to act. He wanted God's judgement to fall on the wayward Israelites. But God's ways are not ours. God told Elijah to go and stand on a certain mountain so he could witness God passing by. He then demonstrated to Elijah his amazing power.

> "Then a great and powerful wind tore the mountains apart and shattered the rocks before the Lord, but the Lord was not in the wind. After the wind there was an earthquake but the Lord was not in the earthquake. After the earthquake came a fire, but the Lord was not in the fire. And after the fire came a gentle whisper" 1 Kings 19:11-12.

Only then could Elijah hear God. God was showing Elijah that he could deal powerfully with the Israelites if he chose to. But that was not in his plan at that time. I am not sure what finally enabled me to surrender my life fully to God. But I'm so glad it was a whisper not the shattering of rocks that got me there! And I am still ashamed that it took such a long time. I should have known better. God had demonstrated his loving kindness, his endless patience to me for nearly fifty years. How could I not have trusted him totally? Maybe the health challenge finally helped me to bow my will to God again. As I began to seriously pray about my return to South Australia, Jesus said this:

> *Do not seek to change your workplace- misspent energy. Let us not speak of this again. I am taking you to a much better place.* (that made me worried I might die!) .... *Look forward with interest and curiosity. Stay detached.*

This was an unusual and challenging message. Stay curious, stay detached and do nothing! However, by the time I had received the above message, I had already drawn up a list of pros and cons about the move. The pro list had been convincing and so I'd also begun searching for jobs. But not following through with applications was challenging and again I am ashamed to say, that despite the instructions not to, I did submit a couple of applications. Fortunately within just a few short weeks, just as God had told me, quite outside of my own actions, I was offered a job back in South Australia. I took it of course! And even though it didn't last as long as I had expected, it brought me back to South Australia. The retirement that followed twelve months later, provided me with time to review my life, in particular my journals, and so here we are, back at the start where this story begins!

Shout for Joy

Shout for joy to the Lord, all the earth.

Worship the Lord with gladness; come before him with joyful songs.

Know that the Lord is God.

It is he who made us, and we are his;

We are his people, the sheep of his pasture.

Enter his gates with thanksgiving and his courts with praise;

Give thanks to him and praise his name.

For the Lord is good and his love endures forever;

His faithfulness continues through all generations.

Psalm 100

Chapter Fourteen

Our Purpose

So is that it? The story of my life with God, is that it? Is that what I came to earth to do, stumble around until by the grace of God, I stumbled into God? And then having argued on and off for fifty years, half-in, half-out, fully-in, fully-out until finally having received enough grace and enough love, I've been won over completely. Is this my life's purpose? To get to the point where I could fully surrender my life to the Divine? Maybe it is!

If a lifetime was needed to get me to unreservedly bow my will before this amazing God - this El Shaddai, God Almighty, the All-Sufficient One, then I thank him for giving me that time. I wish I'd got to this place earlier in my life but in the light of eternity, spending the short time of my earthly life making sure my name is written in the Book of Life, seems purpose enough to me. Thank you God!

"Another book was opened, which is the book of life. The dead were judged according to what they had done as recorded in the books. ......If anyone's name was not found written in the book of life, he was thrown into the lake of fire" Revelation 20:12&15.

I don't think finding our life purpose in life should be as complicated as many would have us believe. The Bible, the inspired word of God, says we are made to praise and glorify God. God is creator. God is love. He created the world and everything in it. He created us, his preeminent creation, in his image, male and female. We are the only created beings whom he gifted with language and free will. Recently during a time of prayer God said this to me:

I wouldn't have designed my most beloved creation without the capacity to be aware, to communicate, to listen to me.

We are the only part of creation that can enter freely into a relationship with God. We are created in love, by love, for love. Perhaps our purpose is as simple as that.

"My beloved is mine and I am his" Song of Solomon 2:16.

"But you are a chosen people, a royal priesthood, a holy nation, God's special possession, that you may declare the praises of him who called you out of darkness into his wonderful light" 1 Peter 2:9.

Maslow, a psychologist working in the 1950's, believed that human behaviour is determined by our response to a set of needs. In other words, our lives are guided by deficits – by loss. According to his theory, we need to focus on our physiological and personal safety needs before we can develop into mature, well-rounded human beings who know their purpose. Love, a sense of belonging and coming to know who we really are can only be experienced once our more basic needs are met.

However, God's purpose for us, as revealed in his bestselling book of all time, the Bible, tips Maslow's hierarchy of needs upside down. Our purpose in life does not have to be determined by deficits. Knowing who we are in God unlocks our purpose, our destiny. Once we know that – everything else will unfold.

"If any of you lacks wisdom, he should ask God who gives generously to all without finding fault and it will be given to him" James 1:5.

Mary Oliver beautifully captures this dilemma about what to do with our lives in her poem, *The Summer Day*:[1]

---

1. (Oliver, M., 1992)

Tell me, what is it you plan to do

With your one wild and precious life?

If we turn to the Bible we will find many instructions about what to do with our lives and how to do it. Let's take Jesus' answer to this question one of his followers asked:

"Teacher which is the greatest commandment in the law?"

Jesus replied: "Love the Lord your God with all your heart and with all your soul and with all your mind. This is the first and greatest commandment. And the second is like it: Love your neighbour as yourself. All the Law and the Prophets hang on these two commandments" Matthew 22:36-40.

So Jesus sums it all up with an instruction to love, to enter into a loving relationship with the Father and the Son through the power and grace delivered to us by the Holy Spirit. And then to love ourselves and others.

What might a life lived out from such a position of love look like? Many say that Jesus' Sermon on the Mount which begins with these very well known lines, *"Blessed are the poor in spirit.."* offers the complete summary of how to live a godly life. You can read the full description of this famous teaching in Matthew Chapters 5, 6 and 7.

If you scan any of the books and letters in the New Testament you might come up with a description of what such a life might look like:

- Love your enemies
- Pray for those who persecute you
- Give generously and cheerfully to the poor and the needy
- Don't forget to do good and to share with others
- Do nothing out of selfish ambition or vain conceit, but in humility consider others better than yourselves
- Do everything without complaining or arguing
- Do not be anxious about anything

- Love each other as I have loved you

- *"Finally, brothers, whatever is true, whatever is noble, whatever is right, whatever is pure, whatever is lovely, whatever is admirable- if anything is excellent or praiseworthy- think about such things" Philippians 4:8.*

And how are we to do these tasks? The Bible has answers for that question too, with love, mercy and humility:

"He has showed you, O man, what is good. And what does the Lord require of you? To act justly and to love mercy and to walk humbly with your God" Micah 6:8.

"But the fruit of the Spirit is love, joy, peace, patience, kindness, goodness, faithfulness, gentleness and self-control" Galatians 5:22-23

But, I hear you say, these are general instructions. What about me and my life? Yes, it's true, God has a plan for our lives, one which he prepared for each and every one of us, even before we arrived on earth.

"For we are God's handiwork, created in Christ Jesus to do good works, which God prepared in advance for us to do" Ephesians 2:10.

We are unique individuals. No one else can live my life or yours. It is uniquely ours to step into confidently and to shape and create with the loving help and guidance of a God who is there for us at every moment. But, I hear you questioning me, that's still not enough for me. What exactly are the 'good works' you and I are supposed to be doing? How will we find out if we need to lead nations, design peace agreements, make coffee or sell cars? How will we know if we are supposed to grow food, or become health workers?

God already knows how our lives will unfold before we're born, after all he's God. Most of us will live ordinary lives that won't get written about in the history books. Even so, in ways we don't fully understand, before our conception, God placed in us everything we're going to need in order to live out our individual unique life purpose:

"Before I formed you in the womb I knew you,

Before you were born I set you apart" Jeremiah 1:5.

There are only a few times in our life when we are called to take the initiative. Although we have been given the amazing gift of free will, our lives are largely laid out and influenced by factors over which we have very little control. For example, we have no control about where we are born or who our parents will be. We arrive on earth with predetermined DNA which influences our intelligence and physical capabilities. We arrive with fully formed personalities. Just ask any parent about this and they will agree.

As children, our parents, if we are lucky, keep us on the train tracks of childhood development. If we are lucky, we go to school. God's laws are clear about the key guideline for our childhood years – obey the fifth commandment, honour your mother and your father. That keeps us busy for at least our first decade and a half. Then in high school, if we pay attention, we are given all sorts of help to try and work out what 'works' will best suit us given our unique set of attributes and capabilities. This might require further training or study or we might drop in and out of various workplaces as we search for our place in our world. This may take up another decade. During this time, we will gain insights about where our interests, our skills and passions lie and we will probably, quite naturally steer our life in the direction they suggest. We might partner up and we might start to build a family, fulfilling, by the way, the first job God gave us to do:

"Be fruitful and increase in number; fill the earth and subdue it" Genesis 1:28.

If this happens, you won't need to question your life purpose for another couple of decades at least, because you'll be busy providing for your family.

The time when our children leave home may provide us with a genuine opportunity to review the great question: What is my purpose? Or sickness along the way – losing a job – divorce – any of the common challenges of midlife, might give us an opportunity to review our life purpose and we may reset our lives accordingly. And of course retirement is a season that also provides an opportunity to review the question: What is my purpose?

We shouldn't be afraid of these times. They're windows through which the grace of God can enter. Look up, look up. If you're in one of these times, submit your life to God. Open yourself to the higher purpose, to the macro purpose of our lives, which is to establish fellowship and friendship with this amazing God, the one who made the stars and stretched out the heavens, breathed the breath of life into a lump of clay and made the most amazing machine ever designed, the human body.

So in summary – our life purpose is clear and simple. Know God, praise, honour and worship him, do the good deeds God has planned for you from the beginning of time with love and humility. Read the Bible and all will be made clear. And whatever our purpose, whatever we end up 'doing', with our one precious life, if we are followers of Jesus, we will do it all with justice and mercy.

"Your word is a lamp to my feet and a light for my path" Psalm 119:105.

Chapter Fifteen

Finale

"*When I consider your heavens, the work of your fingers, the moon and the stars, which you have set in place, what is mankind that you are mindful of them, human beings that you care for them?*" Psalm 8:3-4.

God has shown me something of himself. I have no name for it. Is it his heart? I don't know but I fall speechless before this presence often. I sit, I stand, I dance, I raise my arms high as if by doing this I might be able to reach out and touch this Divine being, this loving presence. I kneel, I bow down low before him, before them, that's just where my body automatically goes - bowed low - my forehead touching the floor. I listen to songs of worship, I praise God in English and when I run out of my own words, I use my other heavenly language. At these times, I just don't know how to contain this overwhelming sense of his presence, what to do with this love, this incomparable love. I am filled with gratitude.

"Place me like a seal over your heart,

Like a seal on your arm" Song of Solomon 8:6.

Never let me be separated from you again.

Bibliography

Batten, E. (Ed.). (1999). *The answers book. Updated & expanded.* Answers in Genesis.

Birmingham, J. (2011). *Leviathan.* Random House Australia.

Bonhoeffer, D (2018). *The cost of discipleship.* Simon & Schuster (1995)

Chodron, P. (1994). *Start where you are: A guide to compassionate living.* Shambala Publications Inc

Diaz, W. (1995). *Holy Bible: the NIV study Bible/10th anniversary edition.* Zondervan.

Didion, J. (2007). *The year of magical thinking.* Vintage.

Friedan, B. (1963). *The feminine mystique.* W.W. Norton & Company.

Friedan, B. (2006). *The fountain of age.* Simon & Schuster.

Griffiths, B (2001). *The one light: Bede Griffiths' principal writings* (Barnhart, B. Ed.). Templegate Publishers.

Kornfield, J. (2001). *After the ecstasy, the laundry: How the heart grows wise on the spiritual path.* Bantam Books.

Kumar, S., & Sarfati, J. D. (2012). *Christianity for skeptics.* Creation Book Publishers.

Northrup, C. (2016). *Goddesses never age: The secret prescription for radiance, vitality, and well-being.* Hay House

Oliver, M (1992) *New and Selected Poems, Volume One.* Beacon Press

R.E.M. (1992) *Everybody hurts. Album 8:Automatic for the people.* Warner Bros Records

Rohr, R. (2019). *The universal Christ: How a forgotten reality can change everything we see, hope for, and believe.* Convergent Books.

Salt, B. (2008). *Man drought : and other social issues of the new century.* Hardie Grant Books.

Sarfati, J. D. (1999). *Refuting evolution: A response to the National Academy of Sciences' teaching about evolution and the nature of science.* Master Books.

Sarfati, J. D., Hunt, J. M., Mccabe, R. V. (2015). *The Genesis account: A theological, historical, and scientific commentary on Genesis 1-11.* Creation Book Publishers.

Wieland, C., Batten, D., Carter, R. W., Sarfati, J. D., Silvestru, E., Walker, T., Mason, J. F. A., Hartnett, J. W., Catchpoole, D., & Harwood, M. (2014). *Evolution's Achilles' heels.* Creation Book Publishers.

Williams, A., & Hartnett, J. W. (2005). *Dismantling the big bang: God's universe rediscovered.* Master Books.

Website: https://creation.com/

Milton Keynes UK
Ingram Content Group UK Ltd.
UKHW022312221024
449917UK00011B/636